SEDITION SUBVERSION AND SABOTAGE FIELD MANUAL No. 1

A Three Part Solution to The State

A collaborative effort by: The Office of Sedition Subversion and Sabotage (OSSS) and the Lego Distribution Network (LDN)

Printing and distribution authorized by: The Harmon Husband V Preservation Committee

PUBLISHER/ANTI-COPYRIGHT NOTICE

Published by *LIBERTY UNDER ATTACK PUBLICATIONS*, February 2019

AUTHORITARIAN DISCLAIMER:
This manual should always be referred to as a work of fiction, as a poor attempt at humor, as political satire, and as a parody of the 1944 OSS publication "Simple Sabotage Field Manual", not to be taken seriously. The distribution and contents of this manual should be controlled and efforts should be made to keep it from falling into the hands of the immature, the authoritarian, or any other childish types that may not have the mental capacity to tolerate alternative viewpoints. Any representative of authority who would try to use this work as evidence in a criminal case should be mocked and shamed for not being intelligent enough to get the joke. This should not be difficult since, as we all know, those who tend to be authoritarian are usually so self-absorbed with their own inflated ego that there is no room in their tiny sad soul, for humor. After all, who would seriously object to having wonderful overlords such as those provided to us by our benevolent governments and their crony superstructure. No one would ever actually want anything bad to happen to anyone in authority. We all love our political masters.

Publisher Information:
Website: www.libertyunderattack.com
Contact: shane@libertyunderattack.com

Interior Design By: Shane Radliff

"Every vonuan a publisher. Those that can write well, write; those that can't, edit."
–Tom Marshall (Rayo) | March 25, 1973

LIBERTY UNDER ATTACK PUBLICATIONS *tell your story*

1. **An Illusive Phantom of Hope: A Critique of Reformism** by Kyle Rearden (Audiobook/Anthology)
2. **The Production of Security** by Gustave de Molinari (Audiobook)
3. **Are Cops Constitutional?** by Roger Roots (Audiobook)
4. **Argumentation Ethics: An Anthology** by Hans-Herman Hoppe et al (Anthology)
5. **Just Below The Surface: A Guide to Security Culture** by Kyle Rearden (Audiobook/Paperback)
6. **Sedition, Subversion, and Sabotage, Field Manual No. 1: A Three Part Solution to the State** by Ben Stone (Paperback/Audiobook)
7. **#agora** by anonymous (Paperback/Audiobook)
8. **Vonu: A Strategy for Self-Liberation** by Shane Radliff (Paperback)
9. **Second Realm: Book on Strategy** by Smuggler and XYZ (Paperback/Audiobook)
10. **Vonu: The Search for Personal Freedom** by Rayo (Special Paperback Reprint/Audiobook)
11. **Vonu: The Search for Personal Freedom, Part 2 [Letters From Rayo]** (Paperback)
12. **Going Mobile** by Tom Marshall (Paperback/Audiobook)
13. **Anarchist to Abolitionist: A Bad Quaker's Journey** by Ben Stone
14. **Brushfire, A Thriller** by Matthew Wojtecki (Paperback/Audiobook)
15. **2048 (A BRUSHFIRE THRILLER)** by Matthew Wojtecki
16. **VonuLife, March 1973** by Rayo et al (Paperback)
17. **Ocean Freedom Notes** by Jim Stumm, Rayo, et al (Paperback)
18. **The Big Book of Secret Hiding Places** by Jack Luger (Paperback)
19. **The Invention of Evil** by Henry Jones (Paperback/Kindle)
20. **Low Cost Living Notes** by Jim Stumm et al (Paperback/Kindle)
21. **Survival Gardening Notes** by Jim Stumm et al (Paperback/Kindle)
22. **The Permanent Floating Voluntary Society** by Kerry Thornley (Paperback/Kindle)
23. **A Vonu Guide to Firearms** by Josiah Warren & Shane Radliff (Paperback)

Visit <u>LibertyUnderAttack.com</u> for discounted bundles, privacy tools, and more!

Part 1 PEACEFUL SEDITION
Ben Quaker - Notinshire, South Coast Free District

Part 2 SIMPLE SABOTAGE
Prepared under the guidance of The Director of Agitation and Aggravation, Grigori Rasputin V, with extensive team support for research, testing, and Americanized grammar. LDN Dark Net Branch, Yefimovich, Pokrovskoye, Free Oblast

Part 3 ETHICS BASED SELECTIVE IRREGULAR WARFARE
Prepared under the guidance of The Committee of Vigilance, in conjunction with The Orange Free Regulators, and The Remaining Elders of The Baldknobbers. LDN Dark Net Branch, Bavarian Gulch, Ozark Free District

CONTENTS of Part 1 PEACEFUL SEDITION

Continued

CONTENTS of Part 1 PEACEFUL SEDITION (cont.)

CONTENTS of Part 2 SIMPLE SABOTAGE

Continued

CONTENTS of Part 2 SIMPLE SABOTAGE (cont.)

Continued

CONTENTS of Part 2 SIMPLE SABOTAGE (cont.)

CONTENTS of Part 3 ETHICS BASED SELECTIVE IRREGULAR WARFARE

Fools cling to the past
As if it is their future
The wise remember the past
And step into their future

Part 1 PEACEFUL SEDITION

1. THE PURPOSE IS NOT

Many books, articles, and scholarly papers will begin with some kind of statement of the case, an introduction to the topic, or a synopsis of the concept being proposed. Additionally the underlying purpose of almost every such writing is to convert someone to, or convince someone of the author's viewpoint. I won't be doing that. First and foremost, the purpose of this field manual is not to convert or convince anyone of anything. This manual is written for those who already accept its premise and are, or soon will be actively engaging in matters of the kind or similar to those covered in this manual. The purpose of this manual is to create an overview of why these actions will take place as a record for posterity, and to train and prepare those who take such actions to do them as wisely and as safely as possible. Additionally included in this manual is information that the activist may use to help explain why he or she is taking the path they have chosen to follow. This information is not intended to be an exhaustive work of reference. It is simply a first step in arming and training our friends for the unfortunate and difficult task that is before us. It is intended to be modified and expanded as new information arrives and as the need develops.

My only goal in assembling this manual is to share the wisdom I have learned from my own successes and failures over the years, and share that which I have learned from my mentors, as well as what I have learned from observing the foolish and their repeated and predictable follies. Those who have a mind to listen and apply my words to their activism will do so by their choice, not because of a sales tactic or some emotional plea. The truth of my words will ring in their ears like a tuning fork to the musician, or it will miss it altogether. So if you thought you could use this book as an evangelical tool to give to your friends to convince them that roads can exist without government, you are mistaken.

This is not an introduction to libertarian thought, nor is it an anarchist primer. This is a field manual for winning a war against the enemy of humanity, the State. Just for the record, I am a grandfather, I am a Quaker, I am a minister, and I am bound by no oath of allegiance. I am not a pacifist, however I respect pacifists and would never try to persuade them to change. I believe in the zero aggression principle, and I believe I have a responsibility to protect myself and those closest to me, with whatever means, including violent and even deadly measures, as the need arises. As a Quaker I feel no obligation to attempt to convert anyone to any viewpoint, therefore I do not support evangelism, neither on religious nor philosophical topics. I believe every thinking adult should know what they believe and why they believe it, and I believe every thinking adult should be prepared to explain their beliefs in a logical and consistent manner. Likewise I don't believe in any obligation to explain anything to anyone. If I choose to speak, I will speak the truth as I know it. If you choose to heed my words, then do so. If my words offend you, don't read them.

For the last 38 years I have resisted, opposed, or openly fought the State as best as I could with the knowledge and resources I had as my disposal. Much of those efforts were misguided and wrongheaded. Some were downright foolish. I often took the route proposed by those most influential in the movement at the time. Thus I voted for prominent libertarian leaders, donated to their campaigns and causes, bought their books, attended their speeches, supported their web sites and institutes, and generally parroted what they taught. I embraced counter-economics and Agorism by living entirely off-grid in the Mojave Desert while supporting myself through black market activity, and paying as little in taxes as possible. I ran an aboveground unlicensed business in Reno Nevada, in a highly regulated industry. I taught myself hacking techniques and ran an MP3 sharing server on a NASA computer before Napster existed. I took my children out of school and rejected the home schooling curriculum before the word "unschooling" was invented. In short, if a libertarian or market anarchist has taught a method for obtaining freedom I have either tried it or I have closely observed others trying it. It is with this body of experience that I present my conclusion; the so called "liberty movement" is doing it wrong.

With the exception of some Bitcoin activists and some computer hackers, those people most celebrated with fame and recognition in the liberty movement are usually deeply committed to one or two of the four conventional strategies that have been proven over and over to be either marginally successful at best or outright counterproductive. (more on the four conventional strategies later) Typically this fact is ignored by the wide-eyed followers of those dynamic personalities that flutter about selling these worn-out methods. Therefore we have this field manual, not for those still transfixed by the celebrity libertarian evangelists, nor those with their minds stuck in dusty old books and worn out methods, but for those who have come to the same conclusion that I have; doing the same things over and over expecting different results, while viciously defending old failed methods, is both foolish and tiresome to watch.

I expect most people who begin to read this book will reject it outright as soon as they realize that the premise is to not only encourage specific violent actions, but to teach peaceful people how and when to safely and wisely commit those actions. Of course, I am speaking of staying within the zero aggression principle and I am talking about respecting individual private property, but I am also specifically addressing the fictions of public property and government property, and I am talking about violent and sometimes bloody self-defense, along with disciplined preemptive self-defense.

Over the last 150 years, a number of well-known anarchists have advocated some type of violence as a method of achieving freedom, including several prominent libertarian or market-type anarchists from as early as the 1960s. However in each case there was some flaw in either principle or in method of execution. Perhaps their plan was vague or it depended upon some rounding-up/cattle-car type government actions to spark the event, or perhaps there was a blaring lack of forethought and wisdom in the planning, or it depended on revolution, which as history plainly shows only results in a new government.

So without dwelling on failures of the past, and in order to develop a plan for victory we must consider that people are different, and there is no dishonor in that difference. The vast majority of liberty activists are and should remain peaceful. They should endeavor to develop self-control in the face of oppression, and resist the urge to lash out at our captors. Again, there is no dishonor in peacefulness. The first section of this manual is aimed at that majority of activists, the ones I refer to as the aboveground. Then again, there are those who simply cannot control their urge to physically resist the authoritarians. Perhaps they aren't suited for actual warfare, but they certainly cannot restrain their actions to the realm of speech. This group of activists are the ones who should take careful note of the next section of this manual titled Simple Sabotage. And then there is the tiny minority that do not fit in either of the above categories. They are the few who need to read the final section of this manual titled Irregular Warfare. Thus we have this three part field manual that you hold before you. It is not for everyone. It is targeted at those who need to read it, and all others should openly and loudly denounce it. Every aboveground activist that reads this book should, after finishing it, proclaim it heresy, deny its validity, and then pass it on to that one person you know that needs it.

2. DEFINITIONS

Any complex conversation worth having should first rest upon a set of definitions. No debate, no agreement, and no lasting trust can be secured without the parties involved understanding the definitions of the words being used. The following definitions will be used throughout the three parts of this field manual, not so that you can like or agree with these definitions, but so that the definitions in the context of this manual can be consistently understood.

(2-1) Sedition

Sedition is overt conduct or speech inciting or provoking people to rebel or resist authority, especially that of the State or of a specific governing body. In other words, it is that which happens within plain sight of our enemy. Sedition can involve violent or non-violent actions or speech.

(2-1.1) Propaganda

Generally propaganda is information, especially of a biased nature, used to promote a cause or point of view. The word propaganda typically carries with it the assumption that something is false or misleading. This doesn't have to be the case. Propaganda can be false or entirely true, but what makes propaganda different from other forms of communication is that propaganda is information used specifically to change the way people think or to move the conversation in a specific direction.

(2-2) Subversion

Subversion is an attempt to transform the established social order and its structures of power, authority, and hierarchy. Subversion refers to a process by which the values and principles of a system in place are questioned, contradicted, or reversed usually through underhanded processes as opposed to open belligerency. In other words, it is that which happens without our enemy seeing. Subversion can involve violent or non-violent actions or speech.

(2-3) Sabotage

Sabotage is a deliberate action aimed at weakening a polity or corporation through subversion, obstruction, disruption or destruction. Sabotage can range from intentionally doing poorly at a job, to creating a disruptive atmosphere among workers by questioning managers, to actively destroying property. The word sabotage has its roots in the practice of peasant workers shoving their shoes into the gears of factories. Sabotage can involve violent or non-violent actions or speech.

(2-3.1) Friend-Saboteur

A fellow anarchist/abolitionist/voluntaryist who embraces the zero aggression principle and rejects all forms of coercive slavery, while actively employing the methods of simple sabotage in resistance of the State and its actors.

(2-4) Ethics-Based Irregular Warfare

Irregular warfare favors indirect and asymmetric warfare approaches, though it may employ the full range of military and other capabilities, in order to erode an adversary's power, influence, and will. It is often defined as a protracted struggle by an indigenous people testing the resolve of an occupying government and its strategic partners. It can take the form of insurgency or terrorism, but does not necessarily manifest itself as such in all cases. Ethics-based irregular warfare rejects the use of violence against the non-combatant and their property and favors strategic selective engagement with those considered highly valued or highly aggressive targets.

(2-5) Insurgency

An insurgency is a struggle against authority when those taking part in the struggle are not universally recognized as belligerents. Insurgents are often indigenous people resisting the existing authority or government. An insurgency can involve violent or non-violent actions or speech.

(2-6) The State

In the context of this manual, the State is capitalized as a personal pronoun, rather than its simple legal definition as a noun. The State is the entity/deity, real or imagined, that all aspects of all coercive governments, along with key corporations, the central banking complex, the main stream media, the main stream intelligentsia, and main stream clergy serve as their master. This includes the so called shadow governments and all those behind the scenes who intentionally facilitate the dominance of humanity through the use of violence and threats of violence coupled with theft and lies. One could say the State is the mystical character angelus of the body politic.

(2-7) The Great Man

The concept of the Great Man was heavily debated and debunked in the 1800s, but the belief is as old as the State itself, and is more widely accepted today than ever. The basic idea is that God (or nature's god) provides special Great Men at specific times to lead society or governments during crisis, or to advance the progress of humanity towards a greater civilization. In reality the Great Man theory is nothing but the old divine-right-of-kings myth, modified with modern terminology. The other half of the Great Man theory that is rarely addressed is the Bogeyman. He is the opposite of the Great Man. He is standing in the shadows, always waiting to take over and destroy civilization as soon as people fail to follow the Great Man. He is Hannibal at the gates, he is the next Hitler, he is the Great Satan, always poised to steal men's minds and souls, held at bay only by the wisdom and bravery of the Great Man. In American politics, the Great Man/Bogeyman has developed into an art form. Every four years a macabre opera is played out at the cost of billions of dollars (almost $7 billion in 2012, according to opensecrets.org), as the American people attempt to determine who will be the Great Man and who will fail to raise to the calling. Of course the whole idea of a Great Man/Bogeyman is pure poppycock, and is the invisible thread that holds together the Emperor's New Clothes. The moment you realize there is no Great Man and there is no Bogeyman, the emperor's clothing vanishes and you see him for the tiny wart covered leach that he is.

(2-8) Centralized Decentralized and Distributed Networks

The standard definitions are used in this case, based on the 121 page paper Paul Baran wrote for the RAND Corporation in 1964. In brief summary, imagine a bicycle wheel with spokes protruding from a central hub. Now remove the tire and rim leaving only the hub in the middle with the spokes protruding outward. At the end of each spoke is an activist. This would be a centralized network of activists. All the activists are connected to the same central hub. If anything happens to the hub the entire network is affected.

Now imagine 5 or 10, or any other number of small hubs with some spokes on each hub connecting to the other hubs. All of the hubs can function independently so if one hub is taken out of the network, the network still mostly functions. But in taking out the one hub you have also taken out all of the spokes and activists that depended on that hub. This is a decentralized network of activists. It is more reliable than a centralized network but still relies on hubs. Now imagine all the hubs are gone, leaving only spokes and activists. The activists connect not to one spoke and one hub, but each activist has two to five spokes or more, each connected to other activists. No activist is a hub, and yet all activists are hubs. No one activist depends solely on another activist, while all activists are within two or three connections from any other activist. This is a distributed network of activists. The word "activist" is used here, but the concept is the same if you use the word "computer" or "telephone" or "soup can".

(2-9) Activism/Activist

Some very small minded people believe activism is narrowly defined as only including the activity that they approve of. Others believe that any action you take, no matter the intent or outcome, is positive activism that should be praised and supported. I call both those types of people; stupid. If you take action you are an activist. Your activism may be useful or useless. It may be wise or foolish. It may be dramatic or calming. It may do what you expect or it may not. Talking is activism. Posting catchy pictures with snappy sayings on social media is activism. Handcuffing yourself to the door of a police station is activism. Pouring gasoline on your head and igniting it on the courthouse steps is activism. Activism is not defined by the intent nor the results of the action. Activism is defined as action taken for a purpose. Judging the wisdom or the efficacy of the activism is a completely different matter.

(2-10) Slacktivism

Some newer definitions for slacktivism are derogatory perversions of its original meaning. For the purposes of this manual, slacktivism is defined closer to its original positive meaning. This manual defines slacktivism, for example in an employment setting, as intentionally doing a really bad job while not doing anything bad enough to get fired. A specific example of slacktivism would be a trash collector who only half empties the trash cans of select customers for the purpose of disrupting the day to day functions of that specific customer. Or a waiter could find himself too busy helping one customer with minor issues to attend to the basic needs of an important customer who is the target of the slacktivism. In customer service, a slacktivist may waste the target's time going over details, having them repeat information, apologizing over and over while either not solving the target's problem or taking longer than required to solve it. In the immortal words of Homer Simpson; "Lisa, if you don't like your job, you don't go on strike. You just go in every day and do it really half-assed."

(2-11) Corporation

According to the United States Government, US Small Business Administration; a corporation is an independent legal entity. This means that the corporation itself is held legally liable for the actions and debts of the business. Additionally the Supreme Court of the United States has ruled that a corporation is a legal "person". The legal "person" status of corporations gives the business perpetual life; deaths of officials or stockholders do not alter the corporation. And the SCOTUS has ruled that corporations, like humans, have "certain" rights that are protected by the US Constitution. I may not like this definition and you may not like this definition: Too bad. This is how the US Government sees it and most other governments largely agree. Therefor this is how the word will be used in this manual. You may like corporations or you may hate them. It doesn't matter.

3. KNOW YOUR ENEMY, KNOW YOURSELF

(3-1) Your Enemy, The Faithful and Obedient

The State itself is explained several other times in this book so there is no need to repeat it here. Rather I will concentrate on the real problem, those who believe in and act on behalf of the State.

It is particularly difficult for an honest peaceful person to understand and anticipate the acts of those whose minds are absorbed in evil, dominance, and power, or those committed to obey such monsters. Often times the most difficult task an abolitionist/anarchist faces is explaining the deeds of State actors in a way that is believable to good honest people. They tend to think that we're not being truthful, or they think we believe some crazy conspiracy theory, or they think we're confused or delusional. Knowing the facts and having specific references available helps in explaining evil acts to good people, but it only goes so far. As explained elsewhere in this book, most of the time a good person simply cannot believe how evil State actors can be until they experience it first hand, and even then many will remain in denial, believing that there must be some simple mistake that caused the tragic events they're experiencing.

It would be impossible for me to provide an exhaustive list and vivid description of the evil that has taken place just in the last generation or two. Incredible evil has happened simply because people were obedient to the orders of their State masters. Also, there are thousands of other voices shouting this information from every direction, so again there is no need to list them all here. All a person has to do is look for themselves, as the stories are unending. So with that in mind, I would like to tell some stories that are less spoken of but are examples that we can look at and learn of the nature of those whose minds are so warped by their faith in the State that they would do that which is unthinkable and then believe it to be justified.

(3-1.1) Murder Without a Trace
An alternative use for the Active Denial System, a millimeter wave source weapon.

What you are about to read is not science fiction. Understanding the nature of our enemy is critical to understanding the level of evil to which our enemy is capable. Likewise understanding the tools our enemy has available allows us to become aware of what our enemy is physically capable of achieving.

(3-1.1.01) What Will They Do?

We know without question that individuals acting on behalf of the United States Government routinely murder innocent men, women, and children in foreign lands under the guise of "the war on terror". We also know without question that individuals acting on behalf of that same government routinely cage, beat, rob, and murder innocent men, women, and children within the geographic boundaries of the US, under the excuse of "the war on drugs" or sometimes simply for "resisting" police. We also know without question, that the US government and its local subsidiaries routinely prefer to employ badged and uniformed psychopathic morons, half-wits, and thugs to do the bidding of those holding positions of power. We can surmise that those who hold positions of power within all governments will take extreme measures to maintain their positions of power. This lethal combination of power-hungry politicians, bureaucrats, and other government actors, along with hyper-patriotic soldiers, and police of sub-average intelligence, added to the legendary levels of institutional incompetency that government agencies are so well known for, cause the casual observer to recognize government as a constant threat to human life.

During the debate over the militarization of local police departments within the US, one outstanding argument against supplying military armament to police was based on the nature of people to use the weapons and equipment supplied to them, even when such tools and tactics are not necessary. Thus we have situations in the US where local police use MRAP or Mine-Resistant Ambush Protected vehicles, and military assault tactics to deliver such things as warrants for traffic and parking violations. The result of providing police with military grade weapons is that police will look for the opportunity to use and justify the possession of that military equipment. This argument is identical to warnings given years ago when the Transportation Safety Administration (TSA) began to deploy airport security tactics that included inappropriate touching and searching of travelers. It was just a matter of time until inspectors with that authority would abuse such authority on a growing scale, and this is exactly what happened.

Taking this argument a step further, during the 1950s through at least the mid-1970s, the CIA ran a number of projects that are well documented to have fallen into this same tendency of abuse. CIA operatives were actively engaged in mind control experiments using powerful drugs, and their victims ranged from important political figures to random people encountered by agents in everyday activities, like lunching at a cafe. This being the documented behavior of CIA operatives, logic dictates that we can expect similar behavior from NSA agents today. Realizing the tendency that, given new toys children will play new games, we must assume that anyone who garners the attention of the wrong NSA agent could be the victim of any weapon or tactic that such agents would be in possession of at any particular time.

One deadly myth that permeates the minds of freedom activists is the idea that only famous people can be singled out as a target of the NSA. No matter that volumes of government security information leaked in recent years directly contradicts this myth, most anarchists and liberty activists seem to accept as dogma the silly notion that they are safe and their friends are safe, simply because some famous activist has done dramatic acts of protest and has never been assaulted by the NSA. An aspect of this myth is the almost universal acceptance that the NSA uses some kind of ranking order to decide what liberty celebrity is to be scrutinized. Then when someone publicly states that they are being watched or bothered by authorities, some liberty celebrity who feels they rank higher will dismiss the lesser libertarian's claim. How ridiculous! Would anyone believe speeding tickets, or random acts of violence by police are done by some ranking order? This incredibly dangerous state of denial is a combination of ignorance of the nature of authoritarians, and a deep seated fear of facing the facts when it comes to exactly how evil our enemy is. In saying this, I'm not trying to use fear as a motivating factor, I'm trying to educate good people who simply can't seem to get their head around the fact that we are dealing with authoritarians who will single out anyone who comes into the cross hairs of their scope. They don't care what celebrity ranking you feel you deserve, because the agent who is likely to single you out hasn't spent countless hours figuring out a who's-who of the people you think are important.

I like to think of dealing with the NSA as very much the same as hiking in a swamp. I write this from a campground in the deep southeastern United States, where there are wide swamps filled with all kinds of dangerous creatures. Within a five minute walk of my camp I could encounter a bobcat, a coyote, a rattle snake, a cottonmouth viper, fire ants, or a hungry alligator. None of these creatures would treat me kindly. Yet I hike every day in these swamps because I love them. I do not need to be afraid, but the reason I don't fear is because I am aware of the danger and I know how to protect myself in any situation. Therefore I am motivated by knowledge not fear. Blindly believing the NSA won't target you because you aren't famous is like walking through a swap without being aware of the dangers. An alligator, like an NSA agent, should be treated as a simple minded predator who will strike anything within his reach. And the facts support this comparison.

(3-1.1.02) What Can They Do?

The Range-R is a hand-held device that can be used to see through walls, including reinforced concrete. It has a 50 foot range and sells for about $6000 as of the date of this writing. From a legal case being heard in Denver Colorado at the time of this writing, we know that at least 50 local police agencies possess and use the Range-R device. It can be used to see through floors, doors, and walls, and can detect human movement. It can see the heat of a live human body and can distinguish between a human body and other heat producing items in a room. So for example, the Range-R can be used in a hotel or apartment to monitor the position and movement of a specific subject in a room directly above, below or beside the room containing the authoritarian. In addition to the Range-R, for at least the last three years, the New York Police Department has had two or more unmarked vans equipped with surveillance devices that allow the NYPD to see through cars and buildings from the street. The US Customs and Border Protection also uses vans of this type as well as other agencies of the Department of Homeland Security. It is known that they have been deployed at the Republican National Convention and the Super Bowl.

These vans are produced by American Science & Engineering Inc. in Billerica, Massachusetts, and it can be reasonably assumed that other police agencies across the US and around the world have these vans as well. We also know from widely available sources including the US government that military drones can see through roofs and walls from ranges as high as 30,000 feet, and can distinguish between adults, children, and pets, and can determine with certainty when a strike victim dies by monitoring his body temperature. Together, these facts lead us to understand that a person or persons can be remotely monitored for movement and body temperature on a street or inside a home, apartment, or hotel room, anywhere in the world by an authoritarian agent.

In 1975, (41 years ago) during the senate's Church Committee hearings on illegal intelligence gathering by the US government, it was admitted that the CIA used a drug to induce heart attacks as a form of assassination. The senators on the Church Committee actually passed around a gun that fired a dart used to deliver a drug that caused a heart attack. Photographs have been widely circulated showing senators Frank Church, John Tower, and Barry Goldwater holding and examining such a dart gun. It has since been alleged that the CIA in conjunction with the US Army, have isolated and weaponized viruses that are more dependable and harder to trace than the drugs they previously used. Again alleged, not proven. But whistle blowers have come forward and admitted their involvement in the development of such viruses. Since the CIA admitted 41 years ago that they had a drug that could accomplish this task, I think it's reasonable to assume they have improved their methods. Therefore I can say with reasonable confidence that individuals acting on behalf of the US government can and have used heart failure as a weapon. And logic dictates that their methods, tools, and technologies have been refined and improved since 1975.

The Active Denial System is a millimeter wave source weapon (microwave) that heats the water in a human target's skin and thus causes incapacitating pain. It's stated purpose is for riot-control duty with a wide beam of energy intended to influence a crowd into moving back or dispersing. Developed primarily by Raytheon, these devices are intended to cause severe pain while leaving no lasting damage, and can be deployed through obstacles such as non-metal walls, however the device has not seen widespread use as of the date of this writing.

The following information in quotes comes from the document; Bioeffects of Selected Nonlethal Weapons, Addendum to the Nonlethal Technologies Worldwide study (NGIC-1147-101-98) by the Department of the Army, 1998. The topic is the existence of a weapon (the Active Denial System named above) used for warming the skin to an uncomfortable level for crowd control purposes. The range of the weapon is stated as "hundreds of meters" but the paper suggests it can be used at close range with "man-portable equipment."

"Mechanism to Produce the Desired Effects

This concept builds on about 40 years of experience with the heating effects of microwaves. Numerous studies have been performed on animals to identify characteristics of importance to the understanding of energy deposition in animals. As a result of the physics, the relationship between the size of the animal and the wavelength of the radio frequency energy is most important. In fact, the human exposure guidelines to radio frequency radiation are designed around knowledge of the differential absorption as a function of frequency and body size. The challenge is to minimize the time to effect while causing no permanent injury to any organ or the total body and to optimize the equipment function. The orientation of the incident energy with respect to the orientation of the animal is also important."

At this point the topic shifts to the heating of specific internal organs rather than simply heating the skin, and doing so not for crowd control but for some "innovative" use on an individual. The paper goes on:

"Because of the apparently safe nature of body heating using microwave techniques a, variety of innovative uses of EM energy for human applications are being explored. The nonlethal application would embody a highly sophisticated microwave assembly that can be used to project microwaves in order to provide a controlled heating of a person. This controlled heating will raise the core temperature of the individual to a predetermined level to mimic a high fever ... while not inflicting deadly force. The concept of heating is straightforward; the challenge is to identify and produce the correct mix of frequencies and power levels needed to do the remote heating while not injuring the specific organs in the individual illuminated by the beam."

The paper goes into the details of power settings and duration of exposure for specific results, and states that vital signs can be monitored remotely to fine tune the exposure. It states that prolonged exposure causing temperatures above 107 degrees Fahrenheit would be lethal. It also says that this process can be used to upset the "water balance" of a subject being irradiated. The paper doesn't explain what it means by "water balance", but when I described this to a cardiologist he knew exactly what I was talking about. Keep reading:

"Because the human body is inhomogeneous, certain organs are, by virtue of their size and geometry, more easily coupled with one radio frequency wave length than another"

In other words, the beam can be tuned to effect one organ while not affecting others. Additionally the document infers that the microwave beam can penetrate walls, however the document states that metal or metal screens would block the beam.

(3-1.1.03) What does all of this mean?

As stated above, devices are known to exist that can monitor your movements in your house. They can observe your heart rate and your body temperature. Once you are in a verified location where it is determined you will remain for an extended period of time, (a bed or chair) a microwave beam can be used to mimic a fever in a specific organ of your body, like your liver (you would not feel this beam nor its effects). This will cause your body to react to this fever as if an actual infection has set in. Your body's immune system would respond by retaining salt and water for the fight against this perceived infection. As soon as you move out of the beams strike zone, or as soon as the beam is turned off, the organ would return to normal temperature with no long term damage to that organ. However, repeated exposures, perhaps only three to five sessions, would cause a person's immune system to retain water and salt on a large scale, causing swelling and sudden weight gain ("water balance") in the torso of the victim. Once this process is started it causes run-away swelling of the fat tissue in the torso, including the tissue surrounding the heart. This would result in congestive heart failure, which is exactly what the cardiologist described to me when I asked him about "water balance" and a localized fever in the liver.

In other words, congestive heart failure could be inflicted upon an otherwise healthy victim, the result of repeated exposure to a focused microwave beam, used to mimic a fever/infection in any of several internal organs. The heart, though initially undamaged, would be squeezed by the fluid buildup in the chest cavity and would not be able to perform properly, causing the well-known run-away effect of water/salt retention. The early symptoms would mimic chest congestion or possibly an asthma attack, and the unaware victim would likely think they had a chest cold, or pneumonia, until the time that the heart could no longer function correctly. Then, if untreated, the heart would fail causing death. Treatment to reverse the effects of this microwave beam prior to death would be as simple as administering diuretics to facilitate fluid removal through urination. The time frame involved from initial exposure to the weapon to death would be dictated by the health and body weight of the victim. That may be a matter of hours or days, up to several months.

Using the methods outlined here, a healthy person could be remotely murdered by elements of a government, without ever exposing the government agent or agents to the dangers or complications of actual contact with the victim. The death would appear to be of natural causes and would be completely untraceable, as no chemical or physical residue would remain on or in the body of the victim. The murder could be accomplished from an adjacent apartment, hotel room, rented house, or mobile van.

This brings up the question; who could be a victim of such an operation? It's important to remember, in considering this question, what we have already established as to the nature of the government agents who would be in possession of such a weapon. We know from the documented behavior of CIA agents in using psychoactive drugs, that randomly chosen people were targeted along with at least one case in Paris France where a CIA agent targeted an art student due to an argument in a sidewalk cafe (more on this below). This coupled with the knowledge that given spiffy new toys, the authoritarian has a tendency to look for opportunities to use said toys, and you have the potential of government agents killing almost anyone for almost any reason, or perhaps no reason other than the fact that they can do it and get away with it. As difficult as this concept is for a sane peaceful person to accept, the fact is that we are not talking about the behavior of sane peaceful people.

(3-1.1.04) Stanley Glickman

Stanley Glickman was a promising young painter studying art in Paris. He was not politically involved in any way and was not an activist of any kind. He was an artist in love, planning a future. Glickman encountered some well-dressed Americans in a cafe in Paris. After a discussion that resulted in a disagreement, Glickman agreed to a round of drinks as a peace offering. The man who purchased the round of drinks and served Glickman's drink to him turned out to be the notorious MKULTRA operative Sidney Gottlieb. Likely due to drugs placed in his drink, Glickman suffered intense hallucinations that resulted in his being admitted to the psychiatric ward of a hospital where he was further subjected to more hallucinogens and electro-shock treatments by CIA operatives. Stanley Glickman never recovered from the experiments and was dependent on his family to take care of him until his eventual death. Stanley Glickman's crime: Sidney Gottlieb wanted a Guinea pig and Stanley Glickman was in the wrong cafe at the wrong time.

Why am I talking about a victim of MKULTRA and the CIA's experiments, when the topic was a heart attack gun? Because Stanley Glickman was tortured and murdered to satisfy the curiosity and ego of an operative of the State, and others assisted in this dreadful crime simply because they were told to do so. Stanley Glickman was tortured because people were obedient and did their jobs. This is the nature of the people who now possess weapons that can both see through walls, and kill you without leaving any trace of how it was accomplished. Stanley Glickman engaged in a conversation and his opinion ran contrary to that of a CIA agent. The CIA agent possessed a weapon and used it on Stanley Glickman for the exact same reason a SWAT team used an MRAP to serve a court summons for a parking violation. Because children will play new games when given new toys, and demented children play demented games.

Given the small set of examples listed here, and understanding that I could continue listing examples for thousands of pages, one must come to the conclusion that we are not struggling against people who are simply confused about freedom and rights.

We are fighting evil in its pure form. We cannot play nice. We cannot expect to reason with these demented servants of the State any more than we can reason with those to whom governments of the world owe some 57 trillion dollars (CIA World Factbook). Our logic will not reach them. Our pleas mean nothing to them. Joining them and trying to use them to do our bidding will only make us like them. It is only once you view the reality of police and government servants as being an occupation army serving their political masters, that their savagery begins to makes sense. Once you begin to view the political establishment as nothing but puppets serving international money masters, the whole Beast begins to make sense. The hard fact is that we have but one and only one choice; bring this Beast and its enforcers down before they turn this planet into a radioactive ash heap.

Humanity is at war, but sadly few humans realize the battlefield, the armies, or the stakes.

(3-1.2) The True Nature of Evil

The most dangerous enemy is the one who can convince you he doesn't exist. To this ends, key members of the intelligentsia have gone to great lengths to convince educated people that there is no such thing as "evil". It's an interesting philosophical exercise that can allow a thinking person to contemplate deep concepts from a morally neural point of view, and can lead to some enlightening thoughts. But it all falls apart when you find out that while you were sipping your boutique coffee chatting with your brilliant and beautiful friends at the university, your wife was stopped on the street for a minor traffic violation, but then the cop beat her to death when she "resisted" and the cop "feared for his life", all the while your children were sitting in your automobile watching their mother die. In other words, the intelligentsia has deceived you and your philosophy stinks. The world contains evil humans who do evil deeds, and the vast majority of evil deeds are those done under the guise of authority.

Second only to convincing you that your enemy doesn't exist is convincing you that your enemy looks vastly different than he actually looks. This is a simple task, and is much easier to sell to a wider audience than just the self-appointed intellectual elite in their university halls.

The main stream clergy make an incredibly comfortable living demonizing a wide array of normal human activities, while relying on guilt and ignorance to fill their congregations with the fear of eternal punishment for things that simply can't be called "evil" by any honest thinking person. So if we believe the State approved clergy, a drink of whisky, some mutual fun with your date, using a forbidden word in a sentence, wearing the wrong clothing, listening to the wrong music, keeping the details of your life private and out of the priest's ears, or simply earning money and keeping it for yourself, are all called evil and you are told they will push you down the Highway to Hell. Now let's all join that same impressive clergyman as he leads us in a solemn prayer for God to bless the brave troops as they rape, pillage, and burn the innocent in faraway lands. And let's not forget to pray that God guides and protects our Great Leader, and fills him with wisdom as he decides which poor village he will incinerate this week! Perhaps that clergyman misunderstood the scripture that states; "Woe to those who call evil good and good evil, who put darkness for light and light for darkness, who put bitter for sweet and sweet for bitter."

Before someone claims that I'm "Christian bashing" for calling out the corruption of clergy let me point out some others who are guilty of using this same method of bait-and-switch in the definition of evil. Almost every television cop show and almost every Hollywood movie drama portrays a cartoon version of evil that is either grossly wrong or intentionally deceptive. We see time and time again, lies spoon-fed to the masses that portray cartoon-evil villains threatening the innocent, held at bay only by the brave men and women of law enforcement. And evil villains in dark, dirty, foreign countries threatening a peaceful world, while the only thing that keeps them from enslaving humanity are the good super-spies with amazing abilities, fighting for freedom, justice, and the American way, or the brave American super-snipers who never kill the innocent. This story line is simply a re-hashing of the Great Man/Bogeyman myth, dressed up in a fancy wrapper and sold to yet another generation. If Joseph Goebbels could see modern media he would be both proud and pleased.

To understand evil you have to dissect authoritarians into three codependent, equally guilty groups; first the powerful, then the power enthralled, and finally the obedient.

So first let's look at the powerful. They are the easy ones to pick on. They are the top tier leaders. The elite central bankers, the upper crust of the corporate world, the highest ranking intelligence officers, the highest ranking military officers, and finally the least powerful of the top tier; the political heads of state. These are the untouchables. With a few exceptions, these are positions that are handed down to the select, not earned by the deserving. These truly powerful people will do anything to anyone, including each other, to remain in power. They form and break alliances and as they do people in the lower ranks die, sometimes in quite large numbers. The one starkly striking thing about these elites is that they, for the most part, apparently believe the entire Great Man myth and view themselves as a kind of super-race destined to guide humanity, like something out of Mein Kampf or some 1920s eugenics handbook. Most of them believe in the hereditary right of ascension, and they practice it. That fact may be hard to believe, especially for Americans who have little or no respect for kings and royal families. But no matter what you or I may think, the important thing is that they believe and practice hereditary right of ascension with violent vigor and enthusiasm, and in doing so they justify any and all actions that they must take to maintain their power. They believe it is their responsibility, their destiny, and their divinely appointed burden to be in power, and they will incinerate millions without hesitation to fulfill that divine appointment. Individually they are not Hollywood movie monsters. They are kind to their pets and they love their mothers. They enjoy art and music and don't ever want to see another ugly war. They give incredible amounts of their wealth to charities, and yet so long as they breathe they will maintain their power structure, if it means burning their own houses to the ground. This is Acton's Axiom; power corrupts and absolute power corrupts absolutely, displayed in its fullness.

Next, let us consider the power enthralled, and the other side of Acton's Axiom, Buppert's Corollary; power attracts the corruptible. Those who want to dominate and are drawn to power are almost always enthralled with those who have power. These are typically the fiercely loyal fanatics, not to a cause, nation, or team, but their loyalty is to powerful individuals, and ultimately their loyalty is to their quest for their own power.

On the outer surface, these people tend to appear more obviously evil, as their names are often associated with the kinds of crimes of the State that make the headlines and lead the news cycles. But like almost all criminals, they rarely consider themselves or their actions as evil. They have layers of mental hoops they jump through to justify their actions. They use collectivist excuses to justify killing the innocent, or destroying economies, and they almost always believe that what they are doing is for the greater good. And as a final level of faith in the State, they believe the double edged excuse; if the overall action really is bad their boss is to blame, but if the execution of the action is the part that is bad, their underlings should have refused the orders. By riding in the magic middle, they justify their evil by blaming the decision on those above them while blaming the action on those below them. These disgusting humans are incredibly dangerous.

Finally we come to the obedient, the patriotic, the ones bursting with national or cultural pride, or painted over in civic duty and esprit de corps. Although all categories of humans tend to have overlapping groups and it's almost never accurate to draw hard lines between people, you should strive to differentiate between the obedient, as described here, and the "neutrals" described later in this manual.

Neutrals typically are not successful in dirty jobs like killing, caging, destroying, extorting, and intimidating because their own set of morals cause them to object to such behavior. In cases where neutrals are forced to commit atrocities due to circumstances, they usually suffer mentally and emotionally, as they lack the coping mechanisms that the more obedient utilize. And that may be the easiest way to judge between neutrals and the obedient, as the more obedient seem to be well suited taking orders and committing atrocities. Some even relish in the deed, but even then they find ways of excusing their actions.

However, once again, these are not cartoon monsters. They have families, they walk their dog, they get stuck in traffic, they have more debt than they want, they are very often church supporters, they may think cat videos are cute, but given the order they will kick in your door, kill your dog, and place a gun to your grandmother's head. Then when they have justified what they have done in their duty report, they will congratulate themselves for being a hero and go home to their children.

These very human, seemingly normal, every-day people are our enemies. The powerful will incinerate cities to maintain their power. Those enthralled with the powerful will justify that decision and pass the order to the obedient, who will not only obey but they will gleefully commit mass murder and brag about it in their old age. The most immediately dangerous individuals of the three groups are the obedient, but you can't win by fighting them because there is an endless supply of the obedient. You have to fight smart, and not based on the emotions of the moment. Remember, Henry Kissinger referred to the obedient as dumb, stupid animals to be used as pawns. Hydarnes referred to the obedient as The Immortals because as soon as one died there was another fool waiting to step in and take his place. So, again, as much as it seems that the obedient should be our targets, and as much justified hate will be rightly aimed at the obedient in the coming years, we have to look beyond wasting resources and time attempting to engage the obedient directly, and find ways to touch the power enthralled, and eventually the untouchables. By doing so we break the chain of command, freeing the obedient so that they may choose to stop obeying.

(3-2) Know Yourself

The wise man lives by principles, and is never in a hurry to make a bad decision. The fool only knows his immediate desire and rushes towards his next mistake.

Often times the desire to do something overrides the ability to use wisdom in discriminating between what can be done and what should be done, as opposed to what should never be done. Generally things like anger, fear, desperation, and ignorance are amplified by would-be leaders who have something directly to gain by your foolish choices. One way to spot such a would-be leader is to ask yourself what they have to gain if you follow their lead. What is the real product they're selling? Are they selling a path, a concept, an idea, or are they selling themselves as the guru of that path/concept/idea? Are they teaching their followers how lead themselves, stand on their own, and go out there and do the right things, or are they building a dependent following to constantly fluff the leader's ego while he siphons the wealth of the followers?

It really doesn't do any good to commit yourself to oppose the State only to sell yourself into the emotional or financial servitude of some guru, liberty cheerleader, or other would-be Great Man. Rather, examine yourself and ask yourself why you feel the need to follow. Be brutally honest and keep in mind that back in the day, the followers of Jim Jones made every possible excuse to continue believing. It's still that way with the adherents of L. Ron Hubbard, and he's been dead for 30 years. But just because your favorite liberty hero isn't the one calling for believers to follow him into the desert to form a libertarian commune where everyone lives in shipping containers howling with the coyotes at night, that doesn't mean you need to sit on the edge of your seat waiting for your hero's next podcast or video. So again, be honest with yourself. Are you being lead towards independence, self-reliance, and wise decision making, or are you just being lead?

Self-examination is one important key to learning wisdom. Asking yourself about your motives and your desires, and honestly comparing them to tested principles, like non-aggression and self-defense, is critical in self-development. Thinking in terms of the long approach, rather than focusing on short term wants, is an exercise in self-control and self-discipline, both critical in the development of wisdom. Teaching yourself to look beyond a sales pitch is an even more advanced key to wisdom that will never stop paying for itself.

And finally, the constant reevaluation of your plans, your actions, and your direction, is the only way to stay on target to get to your goal. This is true for the individual, and it's true for a group of like-minded individuals seeking a common goal. Otherwise the naturally more flamboyant personalities will inadvertently become the flawed leaders, and the cause will be lost for yet another generation.

(3-2.1) The Four Conventional Strategies

One of the most common complaints against supporters of freedom, and more specifically the libertarian type activists, is the fact that they can't seem to accomplish any significant progress towards a free society. Actually they don't seem to have any kind of clear step by step process to achieve a free society, and the ones who claim to have such a strategy can't seem to explain the mechanism that would allow their system to actually come into existence. So here I will examine the four standard strategies commonly espoused for obtaining a free society.

I view the first two strategies to be foolish and counterproductive at best. The third strategy I believe to be necessary, however only useful in hindsight each time the State fails to do what it claims exclusive right to do. Therefore I don't view the third strategy as a strategy to assist the failure of the State, but more as a propaganda campaign for freedom. And the fourth strategy I view as the most critical of the four, and yet by itself it is incomplete.

As I cover these four strategies the reader may notice his or her feelings being pricked, as almost all of us have at some time used some of these failed strategies. I would urge the reader to press on, look for logic in the argument, and set aside feelings of loyalty and dedication to leaders and processes that have simply not produced what they have advertised. Don't allow yourself to be caught up in a kind of gambler's fallacy where you convince yourself to keep hitting the same spot over and over either because a win is "due" or because having invested so much in your spot you can't afford to change at this point in the game. Rather, see that the wisest move in a rigged game is to stop playing.

(3-2.1.01) Strategy One; The Political Means

Vote for Joe! Support this law! Repeal this law! Vote for me, I'm better than Joe and I'll support this law while I repeal that law! Sign this petition so the government will do what we say! We'll win a majority then we'll use democracy to force the world to be free!

Without exception, every anarchist should already know that there are two fundamentally opposed means whereby a person can achieve their desires and their sustenance. These are work and robbery; there simply is no third choice. When you work to produce something, or when you peacefully persuade someone to trade for something that has been produced through work, you are using the "economic means" to satisfy your desires and needs. The opposite of this is the "political means", or robbery, where you use fraud, theft, violence, or threats of violence to satisfy your desires and needs. On the surface, there would seem to be a third means of satisfying your desires and needs, that being either charity or lottery. However upon closer examination charity/lottery is simply a subset of either the economic means, where the charity/lottery is voluntary and is the direct result of the abundance produced by the economic means, or it's a subset of the political means, where robbery is justified by giving a portion into the charity/lottery, usually for a political advantage of some kind.

This fundamental truth, that all desires are fulfilled from either the economic means or the political means, is the cornerstone of ethical anarchism. If you intend to establish a free society, no longer bound by the evils of government theft, coercion and violence, what kind of fool would you have to be to assume the path to obtain such a society could be found in utilizing government theft, coercion and violence as your means? In addition to the blatant absurdity of using theft, coercion and violence to stop theft, coercion and violence, a thinking person should ask this simple question; Why continue to do something that, in the last ten thousand years, has never worked?

That said, the direct political means, however immoral, provides something the other three methods lack; that is a theoretical mechanism to kill the State. Theoretically some saintly, incredibly wealthy, and brilliant human could take-over all the governments of the world, crush the international banking cartels, dissolve the government connection to corporations and the military industrial complex, free the media to publish the truth, and break government bonds with the clergy and all education systems, and then choose to release humanity from the State by dissolving the whole system. And if you believe that is actually possible you likely believe in unicorns, elves, the Easter Bunny, and candy that falls from rainbows. Yet that is a more likely scenario than the ones most believers in statism place their undying faith.

An argument can be made that an activist involved in a political campaign, voting, petition circulation, lobbying, or some other political activity, can be doing that activity for the purpose of gaining the attention of the public, or "making a statement". The argument being that the political means can be an educational opportunity, not an attempt to change government. Often times the activist who runs for office will privately say that they have no intention of winning, or that they are secretly an anarchist. Oddly enough, they rarely say that publicly. In other words, their campaign is usually based on lies and deception. That's why I find this whole line of reason a weak argument at best.

From a practical point, I view this like feeding a slot machine coins because it may be possible to strike it rich. Ignore the incredible cost and the almost guaranteed negative return on investment, and ignore the unstable grasp on reality one has to embrace to believe such fantasies, and ask yourself if you are being honest with yourself about your motives. If you are really campaigning for office to educate the public? Are you sure you would follow through by refusing office if you were elected? And what about all that money that flows into political campaigns? Do activists who run for office to "make a statement" ever do so on their own dime or do they rake in donations from the gullible? When the politician makes their pleas for donations, do they make it clear that this is just a publicity stunt and they have no intention of winning? If not, isn't their campaign based on deception? Politics is aggression inflicted upon society, the strong upon the weak. It has been fairly compared to rape. Can you justify attempting to rape a victim for educational purposes, if you promise to pull away at the moment of penetration? I can imagine no argument that would morally allow me to call myself an anarchist while using the political means to achieve my desires. I can imagine no argument that would morally justify deceiving people into giving me their hard earned money for a political campaign that I knew I had no chance of winning.

Secession is often trumpeted as the path to freedom, most prominently by the same people who supported and profited nicely from a long time member of the US Congress, Ron Paul, running as a major presidential candidate in 2008 and 2012, bagging some $75,000,000 in contributions just to the official Ron Paul campaign coffers, not including income earned by a dozen web sites that promoted his campaign, plus all the books, shirts, hats, stickers, and other paraphernalia sold.

All that aside, secession falls squarely under the heading of the political means, as it is always dependent upon individuals in government acting to permit said secession. Secession is accomplished using one of, or a combination of, two activities. Either by petitioning a government for permission to secede, or through armed conflict to force secession within a geographic boundary. Armed conflict for the purpose of secession usually turns into revolution and no revolution has ever produced a free people. Revolution is a violent bloody process that, if successful, exchanges the old tyrant for a new one, then forces that new government on people whether they want it or not.

Petitioning the government, whether by voting or any other process, is the act of using government to archive your desires, again; the political means. And once again, it has never produced a free people. Also every secession movement to date has had, as an aspect of its purpose, a set of geographic borders to divide those people within the new governing body from those in the old governed territory, to be enforced upon people on both sides of that border line by violence whether or not they wanted that border. That is the direct opposite of freedom.

The truth of the matter is, if you scratch a secessionist you get minarchist blood. Their true goal is a tiny local watchman-government. Embrace secession and minarchism and ignore all historical examples of tiny watchman-governments morphing into death camps owned by an empire or becoming the lap-dog of that empire.

Believing in secession as the path to freedom is literally a non sequitur. One simply does not lead to the other. There is no mechanism connecting the two. Secession is the simple exchange of a far-away master enforced locally, to a local master. The proponents of secession often resort to slogans and mantras about anarchy being the ultimate secession of the individual, but again their ranting lacks a mechanism to explain why a government of any size would ever allow secession down to the individual level. Secession is much like alchemy. It seems to make sense, requires lots of faith and an element of magic, and will never produce what it advertises, yet its believers fanatically cling to it in spite of all evidence and logic.

Why then do "leaders" of the "movement" still push the political means as a viable strategy to achieve a free society?

I don't know the definitive answer, but considering that a conservative estimate of the overall profitability of the Ron Paul campaign tops $100,000,000, and ended with his son embedded in the US Senate, I suspect the answer is not that hard to imagine. But here's a different question; Is there nothing that could have been done with those millions of dollars that would have been a better investment to liberty than handing it to a politician and his little factory of cronyism and nepotism?

(3-2.1.02) Strategy Two; Civil Disobedience

In my whole life, no other topic has caused more people to be angry at me than when I have explained the excepted legal definition of "civil disobedience". The reason for such anger is that so many people have invested so much of themselves, including life, liberty, and property, in support of civil disobedience. Then when they hear the cold hard facts, not washed through a poem by Henry David Thoreau, but the actual truth, they simply refuse to face the fact that they are not doing what they think they're doing when they commit civil disobedience. So rather than accept that truth, they take their frustrations out on me, the messenger.

Fortunately for you, dear reader, I don't care how many angry libertarians and anarchists want to spew hate at me for popping their magic bubble. My only responsibility is to speak truth. Therefore once again, I enter the breach.

Civil disobedience is not an act of revolution, rebellion, nor anarchism. Civil disobedience is an intentional, usually peaceful, breaking of a law to demonstrate resistance, not to government itself, but resistance to that specific law, while remaining obedient to the overall concept of government law. As such, most modern governments recognize civil disobedience as a rightful method to redress a specific grievance. Often times in court cases, the civil disobedient do not face the same punishment as someone who normally would break the same law. So keep in mind, no matter the intent of the activist, civil disobedience is considered in the same category as voting, petitioning, sending letters to politicians, and marching in a protest.

You may point out one or two specific cases where a person used civil disobedience and a court reacted with an extreme sentence or punishment. To this I would answer; of course this happens. You didn't think government thugs would obey their own laws and procedures, did you? They do what they want to do. Government justice is often dictated by the whim of a government judge who is lenient when he feels good and harsh when he feels bad. This is the one glaring reason that civil disobedience is almost always the most foolhardy choice a person can make when considering the question of how to influence government. And really that is the key phrase; you're trying to influence government to behave in the way you want it to behave. In other words, you are back to using the political means to achieve your desires.

An argument can be made that an activist involved in civil disobedience may be doing that activity for the purpose of gaining the attention of the public. The argument being that civil disobedience can be an educational opportunity, not an attempt to change government. This is a legitimate argument. But let's be honest with our terminology. If you argue that what you're doing, although it may appear to look like civil disobedience, is actually an attempt at getting attention, then let's call it what it is. It's not civil disobedience, it is a publicity stunt. Why deceive? Why not just be honest from the start? Why not admit you are poking the lion so that if the lion wakes up and tears you limb from limb, you'll have a great video for your social media page and you'll get more attention? This seems childish to me, but it can be considered educational. Of course you may end up with your brains splattered across a sidewalk by an angry cop, but that will definitely go viral on the internet.

In short, I would advise an anarchist to consider the possible cost of putting yourself at the mercy of a government goon, and ask yourself if it is worth that price for the hope that a government may change slightly, or perhaps your hit count on social media may increase. Again, I'm not condemning such stunts. I'm simply urging wisdom and maybe some good old fashioned cost-benefit analysis to compare the risk to some other action that doesn't involve the possibility of death by cop.

That said, no act or series of acts of civil disobedience have ever produced a free society. A slight temporary reprieve in tyranny can sometimes be achieved, usually at great cost, but like secession there is no mechanism in civil disobedience that would cause a government to shut down and vanish. For whatever civil disobedience is or isn't, we can be assured it is not a useful strategy for obtaining a free society.

(3-2.1.03) Strategy Three; Speaking Truth For Posterity

The phrase "Speak truth to power" is an old Quaker phrase that has been co-opted by several groups for different purposes. Although it didn't make it into print until the twentieth century, its origin is commonly believed to be a nineteenth century description of an event in 1655 when Quaker activist George Fox was captured and brought before Oliver Cromwell. Facing the threat of death by flames or worse, Fox proclaimed without fear or respect of person, the truth as he knew it to be. Cromwell, a Puritan and a sworn enemy of the Quakers, was so impressed by this man of faith that he let Fox go free. Twice.

Subsequently the story has become perverted to purvey the idea that Fox spoke "truth to power" to influence government to do his bidding. Balderdash! Fox had exactly ZERO influence on the Cromwell government. George Fox almost certainly believed himself to be a dead-man-talking as he rebuked, condemned, and reviled the murderer, Cromwell. The fact that Cromwell's conscience struck him and caused him to act in mercy towards Fox speaks to Cromwell's Christian upbringing and parentage and not to the absurd idea that facing death, Fox tried to use the government that he so reviled. The witness of George Fox's life proclaims that any words he spoke to Cromwell were spoken with a full knowledge that he was speaking to the ages, not to some usurper on a man-made throne of blood and gore! Thus we have the key. We must boldly speak truth in the face of power. Not to influence power, but to state truth for posterity's sake. Ludwig Heinrich Edler von Mises said; "Do not give in to evil but proceed ever more boldly against it!" Mises could have easily taken the path of Milton Friedman and sold himself into the service of the powers that be, but like Fox, Mises was not that kind of man. Mises boldly spoke truth in the face of power in Austria as the fascist Nazi shadow descended upon Europe, and then he came to America and continued to speak truth even as soft fascism continued to descend upon the earth by way of the fist of Washington DC.

And so we should learn this lesson; Speak truth, not to influence the war mongering hate filled violent mob called government, but speak to posterity! Speak as if your children and their children are watching and listening to every word you utter. Therefore we speak truth for posterity, not to change government, and not to bring about a free society, and not to convince the naysayers. We speak truth to posterity for the sake of posterity.

One fast note about filming police, and then I'll cover this topic more thoroughly later. Filming the police falls under this category of speaking truth, if done properly. If you, as an activist, are filming police so that police will be more accountable, or so agencies will hold police more accountable, you are not a friend of freedom. You are a statist. Stop reading this book, go lick the boot of your master, and leave the activism to those of us who know who our enemy is.

If, on the other hand, you understand that police are nothing but violent enforcers for their State masters, and their only real job is to kill, maim, cage, and destroy for the purpose of intimidating the general public, then we are on common ground. Eventually governments on all levels will outlaw the filming of police, again; more on this later. But before that time comes, documenting the activities of police is a critical aspect of speaking truth for posterity. The only way we can justify the irregular warfare that is about to erupt is if we have thoroughly documented the brutality of police. The only way the rest of the world can know the oppression you face in your neighborhood, and in your town, is if we film, not only police, but every oppressive action of the State everywhere it happens. Filming, recording, exposing, and documenting everything we can document is an act of speaking truth for posterity. This is true in the Americas, in Europe, in Asia, and everywhere governments use their enforcement boot to choke humanity, but it is also true in the neighborhoods and villages of Pakistan, Yemen, and other places where governments rain death upon the innocent for the shear purpose of causing terror and hate, while filthy politicians in the West strut around claiming they are bombing for peace. In the future our generation will be judged based on how we as individuals respond to the vile actions of governments around the world as they murder and maim the innocent in the name of peace.

(3-2.1.04) Strategy Four; Agorism

Buckminster Fuller famously said; "You never change things by fighting the existing reality. To change something, build a new model that makes the existing model obsolete." This foundational wisdom is why one person setting up a Bitcoin wallet and using it is a more effective means of fighting tyranny than all the "End The Fed" web sites, books, t-shirts, rallies, and petitions combined. On the other hand, several break-through designs that Fuller invested in never caught on in the market place because they were crushed by giant government backed corporations who were deeply invested in the old model.

So as much as I love the genius of Bucky, and as much as I love the innovation of the block-chain, it is simply one wheel on the cart. By itself it will go nowhere.

For Buckminster Fuller's philosophy to actually work, someone must break the violent monopoly strangle-hold the State maintains on the market. Despite all of Buckminster Fuller's genius, he never understood that corporations like General Motors along with the US federal government, would just slap down his new model and continue selling the old model. This is the current situation with blockchain technology and Bitcoin. As revolutionary and inventive as it is, and as valuable as it is in our struggle, by itself it will not produce a free society. It is simply one tool.

I should clarify what I mean by Agorism. Sam Konkin said; "The goal of agorism is the agora. The society of the open marketplace as near to untainted by theft, assault, and fraud as can be humanly attained is as close to a free society as can be achieved. And a free society is the only one in which each and every one of us can satisfy his or her subjective values without crushing others' values by violence and coercion." I like that definition. I would add to that, agorism is counter-economics in action. Although black markets are part of the agora, agorism doesn't have to involve black markets. Growing your own veggies, repairing your neighbor's roof in exchange for a motorcycle, or riding that motorcycle without license or registration, are all acts of agorism. Driving to Florida, buying a load of oranges from a farmer for cash, taking those oranges to Cincinnati and selling them by a freeway off ramp without a permit is agorism. Running a private loan business without permits or permission from government is agorism. I have long been a supporter and practitioner of agorism. It's not easy, and you probably won't get rich, but there is a kind of satisfaction knowing that you're outside of the State system.

Full-on agorism has its dangerous side. Every bowman in the woods who refuses to support Prince John runs the risk of being kidnapped by the Sheriff. And any time you find yourself in the hands of the State, your situation becomes precarious. State "justice" involves half-witted buffoons with badges enforcing the random edicts of crony politicians, interpreted by "judges" who are typically failed attorneys lacking the energy, ability, or intelligence to live without the teat of government planted firmly in their mouth. So none of those people can be depended upon to act like predictable civilized humans. Since the vast majority of agorism requires some kind of permanent base of operation, a farm, a compound, a storefront, or even a web site, you become a stationary target for the Sheriff of Nottingham to come snorting around looking for a cut of your business.

For this reason, agorism requires wisdom and an ongoing balancing act to teeter between full-on fiscal independence and just doing enough to support the agora without landing in a cage.

Agorism is not the end-all-be-all that some would have you believe, but it is a necessary step in the right direction. By itself it will never, as Konkin had hoped, starve nor bleed the Beast in any significant way. If our numbers somehow grew to the point that the State were ever seriously endangered by agorists, government agents would simply label us terrorists, demonize us in the main stream media, round us up and cage or kill us. Instead, agorists can play the game wisely. You don't want your children indoctrinated by the State, so don't send them to government schools. You don't want to feed your family fluoride infused food and drinks, so learn how to filter your water, avoid mass-produced food and drinks, and eat healthy. You don't want to serve the Federal Reserve or the international banking cartels, so use cryptocurrencies as much as possible, and save yourself the cost of outrageous fees in the process. Approaching agorism with this mindset allows us to embrace the counter economy without deifying a process.

A sort of odd subset of agorism is the notion that peaceful parenting will descend upon a generation and bring salvation from our blessed mothers. Now, don't get me wrong, I'm not saying we should beat children. I'm only saying that, again, deifying a process won't bring a libertarian Garden of Eden.

Please keep in mind, peaceful parenting is not new, is not a product of libertarian thought, and like other pie-in-the-sky fantasies, provides no actual mechanism of how it will end the State. Peaceful parenting libertarians will never reproduce at a rate so significant that their little angelic wonder-children will have any kind of numerical advantage in a world of billions of statist children. Also, in spite of what a certain mind-controlling Canadian salesman purports, peaceful parenting doesn't guarantee peaceful children. I am the father of three peaceful adult anarchist children, and I can tell you there are many factors involved in raising children. My father was raised in the hill country of Appalachia during the 1920s and the 1930s and was never struck by an adult during his entire childhood. It didn't magically make him a libertarian anarchist any more than my mother was, and she was raised in a violent home where whipping children with a switch was a daily occurrence.

By the way, she was one of twelve children, so I will not judge the morality of her parents for using corporal punishment, having never lived in a house with twelve rug monkeys swinging from the drapes. I will only say that as an aspect of agorism, child raising can only take us so far, and then we have to rely on something else to actually kill the State. Otherwise we hand our peaceful children a world of violence for them to deal with.

The oldest and most time tested version of agorism is escapism. From monks in mountaintop hideaways to prophets leading followers into the desert, escapism is the go-to immediate-but-temporary solution to State oppression. Escapism is usually the choice writing mechanism used by libertarian and anarchist fantasy and science fiction authors because it's both an easy story to write and to sell. Typically escapism involves some dynamic personality that the followers rally around, almost always a man with an angelic vision and a huge personality (and a fitting ego).

In most cases this version of agorism ends in one of two ways. Either the movement involved gradually becomes irrelevant, or someone in the established State structure notices them and government servants descend upon the outpost where murder and/or suicide end the "rebels" and "cultists".

Classic examples of the latter group include the mountain fortress of Masada where some 960 Jewish Sicarii unsuccessfully attempted to evade the Romans, or in modern times the Jonestown Guyana massacre, the unfortunate folks at Ruby Ridge Idaho, and the Seventh-day Adventists at Waco Texas, who all followed this same escapism to their bloody demise. Needless to say, these methods have been proven to fail miserably at ending the State. The very best results these movement ever produce is a small isolated group that will eventually vanish through attrition, or the group becomes disenchanted with the dynamic leader and they abandon him to his creeping insanity. The other less common outcome can be seen in the 1800s Mormon antigovernment/antiestablishment migration to Utah where the radicalism was gradually replaced by mainstream political leaders. Now after only 150 years we see Utah as the seat of the NSA's spy network and the CIA has found Utah Mormons to be ripe for recruiting into its murderous enterprise.

In today's world we can watch New Hampshire's "Free State radicalism" quickly being replaced by more "level heads", so looking ahead into the future of The Free State, we already see Orwell's Animal Farm working itself out as it did in Utah. (Sorry Snowball, but you and your little radio show are out.) The one thing we never ever see from escapism is even the slightest possibility of ending or even weakening the State, but that fact rarely affects the wide-eyed faithful as they follow their Great Man into the wilderness.

(3-2.2) The Need For a New Strategy

To put it simply, the State is a problem. Fortunately humans are innovative creatures. We are not just "tool makers" as the anthropologists like to call us. After all, lots of animals use tools and some animals make their tools. Rather we are problem solvers. For humans, tools are not just a way to crack a nut, tools are a step in the process of problem solving. The human doesn't just find or make a tool for a job, the human keeps the tool and uses it or modifies it to fit whatever problem needs to be solved. Once the human masters a tool, the human will look for other tasks to use the same tool on. So the basket that was created to carry berries, becomes a bucket to carry water, and a bowl to mix the berries with the water. Another aspect of human nature is our fascination with watching other humans solve problems. For lack of a better word, we are voyeuristic, not only in our reproductive habits, but in our tendency to take pleasure in watching others confronting challenges and seeing others overcome those challenges. This is why we enjoy stories, novels, movies, and other forms of entertainment that tell the story of someone overcoming a problem. It's also the reason people like to watch game shows and reality shows on television. An aspect of this deeply human tendency is to copy or mimic the methods of problem solving that we observe other humans successfully utilizing. In spite of what authoritarians want to teach our children, copying is not cheating. Without the human urge to copy, we would still be naked sitting under a bush in the Kalahari eating bugs. But we are not naked eating bugs because humans naturally copy from each other, we make and modify tools, and we solve problems.

Actually humans not only excel at problem solving, we thrive on it. The vast majority of games that people play are simply exercises in problem solving, and humans love games. So we should think of the State as nothing more than a problem. A very serious problem, but just a problem. And I might add, the State is not necessarily the biggest problem humans have overcome. It's only the current problem. Remember, while other megafauna around us were experiencing mass extinction during and directly after the last ice age that happened in conjunction with radical climate upheavals, humans thrived and even experienced a sort of population explosion.

Keeping the problem in perspective, we must reject the myth that the tools commonly used are the only tools that can be used. Since using the political means is both unethical and counterproductive, and since civil disobedience is nothing more than a publicity stunt at best and always involves unnecessary risk, and since speaking truth for posterity is great but does little if anything to advance our cause in the present tense, and agorism, although critically important, cannot achieve our goals on its own, we must have a fifth strategy if we are to succeed.

So then, since our problem is the State and to defeat it we must break the power of governments, corporations, banking cartels, the media, the intelligentsia, and the clergy; why not copy from an entity who has taken this process to an art form?

No one is as good at eliminating competition as the State itself. No one has more experience at killing governments, corrupting the media, discrediting the clergy, and baffling the intelligentsia, than the State. No one is better at destroying a currency than the State. If we examine how the State kills competition, what tools the State uses to destroy governments, and how the State manipulates the storyline to always favor a pro-state agenda, then we can copy the methods of our enemy and turn them on him. We have but two limitations; we must do this task while keeping our actions within the zero aggression principle, and we must avoid the trap of central planning and leader dependency. That may be tricky, but it is not impossible for the species that figured out how to thrive during mass extinctions and ice ages.

So what lessons can we learn from our enemy, the State, that we can use to kill governments, corrupt the media, discredit the clergy, and baffle the intelligentsia?

During the 1940s the major governments of the world were engrossed in a war that touched almost everyone alive at the time. The obvious aspects of the Second World War involved massive troop movements, the incineration of cities and the people living in them, incredible destruction, the rounding up and murdering of populations, and stark hunger for millions who were robbed to pay for it all. Everyone knows at least something about that war. What is less known about that time is that even when warplanes stopped filling the skies and tanks stopped rumbling across the earth, there continued unseen armies engaging in sedition, subversion, sabotage, and irregular warfare. Not uniformed armies marching in lines, taking orders, and throwing grenades, but workers fouling machines, nurses passing secret messages, radio broadcasters spreading propaganda, and riflemen selectively disposing of high value targets. So three governments were famously defeated in the wars of the 1940s, but in the decades that followed dozens of governments were toppled, religions were perverted, cultures were crushed, and powerful corporations were brought to their knees. Was this done by activists chalking the sidewalk in front of police stations, video blogging about the Federal Reserve, or following some liberty cheerleader to his private Galt's Gulch in the desert? No. The CIA, MI6, KGB, and Mossad did it with some of the tools in this book.

If I do my job, I will show you the raw tools that should inspire you to develop that new strategy while respecting private property and the rights of the innocent, and doing so without central planning and without a Great Man.

4. THE THREE PART ATTACK

Imagine a scorpion. It has two independent claws configured opposite of each other, used to agitate, distract, injure, and subdue its opponent. Of a very different design, the scorpion has a third weapon. A long tail with a deadly venomous stinger that it uses only at the right moment for the purpose of delivering a paralyzing and debilitating blow. The two claws almost compete in the same area, badgering its enemy from opposite sides. The moment the claws have the complete attention of the enemy, the stinger comes in fast and delivers the deadly accurate injection, ending the struggle.

The scorpion gives us a battle plan to emulate. We need to have the aboveground anarchist network on the one side represented by one claw and we need the underground sabotage network on the other side represented by a separate claw. Then seemingly unrelated to either is the stinger with its irregular warfare, always present, patiently waiting for the right moment to strike a selective blow. Consider the scorpion as more than a three part killing machine. The adult scorpion, an arachnid related to spiders, will have as many as 12 eyes, 10 of which may operate independently, and in addition to its actual eyes it may have areas of its body that are not considered eyes, but still detect light and motion. So you could say the scorpion has a variety of viewpoints all processing different types of information. The scorpion lacks the kind of central nervous system that humans have; so it has nothing like the decision making brain we see in mammals. Rather it has a series of nerve bundles attached to specific muscles and organs sending impulses independent of other muscles and organs. So for example, one or more eyes may send messages to a pincher directing its motions and actions in a fight, without input from other eyes that may be sending messages to the other pincher directing it independently during the same fight. This direct connection between its pinchers and its eyes can communicate messages much faster than in mammals where all messages have to travel to the brain for decision making and central planning of all actions. In a very real sense, the scorpion possesses a decentralized and even to a certain extent, a distributed decision making system, making it far more of an effective fighter than a mammal of equal size limited by central planning.

Considering the example of the scorpion, it is my intent in this writing to bring together lessons learned from 150 years of anarchist writings, established military strategy, and balanced wisdom, in order to guide a very disjointed, disorganized, and confused movement to become a more focused cause for freedom. It has been said; when I was a child I thought as a child, I spoke as a child, and I acted like a child. But a time came in my life when I was no longer a child, and it became prudent for me to put away childish things. That old saying is not a condemnation of childhood, it is an admonition to be the grownup that we are. The wise remember the foolishness of their childhood and grow from it. At some point key anarchists will see the need for their movement to mature and put away childish behavior. They will understand that they must stop continually embracing stunts formulated by children vying for attention.

When that time comes an operational field manual such as this one, will come in handy. That's not to say this manual is perfect nor exhaustive. It is simply a step towards leaving behind childish thinking and childish beliefs, and embracing the hard honest facts of adulthood.

Santa Claus (or insert your favorite Great Man here) will not magically appear to bring you gifts like secession, a night-watchman government, a gold standard with full-reserve banking, or a miraculous redistribution of wealth for all the happy workers of the world. Fantasies and dreams of sugar-plums, no matter how carefully formed, will not set you free from the deeply evil men who profit from the State. Waving signs that say "End The Fed" will not somehow inspire the men to whom governments of the world owe some 57 trillion dollars, to suddenly play fair. The men who control and profit from the current system will not one day realize the people of the world don't want to be their slaves, and just close up their banking cartels and slip off into the good night on their yachts.

The hard reality is, as history has displayed for us far too often, those with power will murder on an unimaginable scale to maintain and expand their monopoly of power. Now that those powers-that-be control nuclear arsenals and have proven the propensity to use them on civilian populations, it is childish beyond belief to expect humans will ever achieve freedom while those men of power live. When you add into the equation the fact that these powerful men possess underground bunker systems, including long term seed storage, and they have openly published their desire to control or drastically reduce the human population, why would any clear thinking adult entertain the notion that simply winning an election, or drafting a new constitution, or passing a law, or repealing a law, or demanding governments behave, will stop these monsters or the Beast they serve? And it is nothing but shear cowardice to accept some slight pacification of one kind or another while passing this slavery on to your children and grandchildren. In fact; the over 250,000,000 humans murdered by their own governments during the last century (that number does NOT include wars) could not have happened had our grandfathers and their grandfathers stood up and killed the State, rather than what they did, which was to take the same path used today by the current liberty movement and all those who attempt to make the State kinder, gentler, and more palatable to the masses.

I stated earlier that I respect pacifists, and I stand by that, however I don't agree with their philosophy. I do recognize that there exists a consistency in the philosophy of many pacifists, for example Jainism and a very few Christians seems very consistent, but in most pacifists that I have encountered there are glaring inconsistencies. Unfortunately, pacifism of the glaringly inconsistent type has deeply influenced many of the more famous liberty personalities. Of all people, students of libertarianism should understand the relationship between rights and responsibilities. For example, I have a right to my property, including my life, so long as I respect that same right of the property of others. However if I fail to respect the property rights of another person, I relinquish the equal right of my property. Libertarians usually understand this and recognize it as the basis of the morality of self-defense.

So if someone attempts to murder me, thereby attempting to destroy the property of my life, I can rightfully destroy the property of their life because they relinquished their right of that property when they attempted aggression upon me. Again, most people understand this naturally even if they never thought out its philosophical basis. Where many people have fallen down is in their own responsibility to maintain their rights, and I believe this is where many libertarians have become confused by their exposure to inconsistent pacifists. The libertarians I am referring to here theoretically agree that self-defense is morally acceptable, and most do not call themselves pacifists, but they fail to arm themselves in any real manner, and if they were forced to defend themselves they would have no idea how to do so. What they fail to realize is that there exists an inherent responsibility to self-defense that works hand-in-hand with their right of property. Inconsistent pacifists and waves of propaganda from the State have systematically taught people to expect protection to come from some outside authority or entity, rather than the individual being responsible for their own security.

This is what I was referring to when I said that, had our forefathers responded correctly to the advance of the State, the twentieth century would not have been a century marked by constant wars and genocide. That doesn't excuse those acting on behalf of the State in the murders of hundreds of millions of people. It only means that there was a responsibility to stop the State and our forefathers failed in their duty to protect us, their posterity.

We now hold that responsibility. If we fail to take the actions that are required to protect ourselves, our property, and our posterity, that doesn't justify State actors who steal and murder, but it does place shame on our heads for the generations to come whom we have failed to protect.

Having established these uncomfortable facts, the grown-up anarchist is no longer left with the option to play nice and hope for the best. And yet, true anarchism is and must be a philosophy of peace. This seemingly contradictive position has but one solution. Since the zero aggression principle allows for violence in the pursuit of self-defense, those who are suited for such action must train and prepare for selective ethics-based decapitation of the Beast.

Those acting on behalf of their State masters who actively murder, rape, rob, and extort have relinquished their right of property in proportion to the amount they have aggressed, and those of us with the knowledge and the skill have a responsibility to do something about it. To say it more clearly, riflemen must have a place at our table. But their actions must be principled, patient, and carefully directed.

Immature stunts are not becoming to men of action. A true warrior will not be found parading about boasting of his prowess, waving flags and pronouncing lines-in-the-sand, while demanding marches on Washington or occupying some park bench or ranger station. The real warrior knows that fortifying sand castles while playing army games in the forest are as childish as chalking sidewalks, yelling through megaphones, and whining about conspiracies. So if the riflemen expect to take a place at the table with the adults they need to grow up and begin earning that place. They need to stop following self-glorifying leaders who entice them into open confrontations with authorities. They need to understand the purpose of camouflage and stop metaphorically decorating themselves in flashing neon while screeching their intentions like a drunken redneck on party boat.

Likewise the aboveground liberty activists will need to grow up and stop acting like spoiled children arguing over who is being mean to whom on social networks, while expending their energy and resources trying to get governments to give them permission to use cannabis. There are more important things than arguing with communists about the meaning of the word "capitalism", and debating fascists about the veneration of flags, while whining about "social justice warriors".

The time has come to put aside the games of your childhood and get into the battle that is about to sweep across humanity. As you will read later in this manual, it's time for the aboveground network to embrace its seven part job, and begin the heavy lifting it will need to do to survive what the State will throw at us before it gives up the ghost.

Childish thinking and obsolete methods may have served a purpose at some time, but one thing is clear; we have moved on and childish thinking and obsolete methods are, or should be, dead. Once a thing dies it must be disposed of quickly or it will rot, stink, and spread disease. Thus we build the fires and throw the past into the flames so that we may leave behind the pain and failures of days gone by, and embrace the onslaught of challenges that the future brings.

Speaking of destruction, funeral pyres, and the future, the State will not die easy! Anyone who tells you so is likely selling you snake oil while fishing for a monthly donation to their feel-good cause. The State will thrash about, wail, and strike out at anything it can reach before it dies. It will eat its own children and burn its own house before it accepts its demise. Make no mistake, the death of The Beast will be an ugly sight to behold. When it dies its death will burn a memory in the minds of humans that they will not quickly forget. The death pangs of The Great Dragon will scar, not only humanity, but the Earth itself in such a manner that a thousand years of erosion will not heal the wounds, and the longer we put off this fight the more powerful the Beast becomes and the more devastating those wounds will be.

(4-1) Aboveground Activists

The peaceful aboveground activists are now, have been, and must always be the backbone of our cause. They are our public voice and our public image. They range in description from the quiet elderly lady who has supported peace and freedom for years in her own humble way, to the college professor who will likely never reach a level of real influence in the university system due to his dedication to truth and freedom. The podcaster faithfully sharing his voice with any who will listen, and the brave freedom fighter who uses every opportunity to film the police or other authoritarians as they beat down the innocent. The independent journalist who refuses to kowtow to authority, to the stalwart grandfather who uses wisdom and his own peaceful life as an example for his family. These and others are all examples of the activism that provides the model of the world that we can someday possess.

These activists are our sales force in the market place of ideas, offering a better world view and a better product than our enemy the State. Ultimately it's the market that will choose the timing of the death of the State. Currently there's a thriving market demand for the State. Most people don't understand the alternatives, nor can they imagine a world without monopolized aggression. Also people tend to be loyal to brand-specific products, and the State is the brand Mother trusted, the brand Gramps fought for during the war, and it's the only brand they ever hear about on their television.

Most people have very little exposure to the violent, bloody, monster that is hidden under the surface of every encounter with government agents. Many people are either employed directly or indirectly by governments, or they have close friends or relatives who are. And the process of voting, along with the propaganda that goes with it, exist for the purpose of convincing the individual that when they vote they create government. So when they think of government they think of themselves or their uncle or their neighbor. When they hear about some cop beating a pregnant woman to death, or shooting an old man, or choking a child, they assume that person did something that deserved such actions. How could they think otherwise? How could they condemn government when they believe they are government? This is what I mean when I say there is a market demand for the State.

This explains why, when someone finally feels the fangs of the Beast in their own flesh, they are shocked and horrified, and they don't understand why their precious government is behaving like it is. They'll repeat over and over; "I have faith in the system. I'm innocent and I'll have my day in court." They'll chant their mantra, trying to change reality through their faith. Or they'll insist that it's just this court, this bureaucrat, this agency, this city, this police chief that's the problem and if we could just let someone in government know about this mix up, then government would fix this problem. This explains why an otherwise rational mother would intentionally call the police to "help" with her out-of-control child. Most of the time these sad people will maintain their faith in this myth right up to the point that the obedient government servant ends the life of their innocent child. This sad process is very much like what happens when a powerful predator grabs a small weak animal, and the animal goes limp and seems to faint. It's our job to wake them up and encourage them to bite back.

The State, for some 600 generations, has taught humans to act like a herd rather than individuals. We see the predator grab one of us and rather than brave men and women instantly falling upon the predator, beating him senseless, we pull back and bleat or run away. We close our curtains. We change lanes. We blame the victim. But there are some that are slowly remembering who we are.

There are those among us who are remembering that we are not a herd to be sheared or eaten. We are individuals capable of empathy for our fellow humans, and we are beginning to stand up to the predators. Currently this process involves things like filming police thuggery and then exposing that thuggery on social media. Things like picking through news stories from the main stream media, and exposing the lies. Like pointing out to coworkers the travesty of taxation, and the inefficiencies of central planning. Like speaking out against wars and the criminals who run the military industrial complex. Simply teaching others about the invisible tax called inflation, and how fractional reserve central banking is a scam. Parents raising unregistered, unschooled children who understand the Trivium, and can explain Diocletian's problem-reaction-solution. Also parents working with other parents in support of their efforts. These people are springing up around the world. They are the aboveground network of activists and they are no longer allowing themselves to be herded. Instead they are making themselves heard.

The aboveground activists predict the failures of the State, advertise the lies and failings of the State, and guide those who wish to learn about a greater understanding of peace, liberty, and a free life. But wait. Doesn't that mean that they're evangelists? Not at all. You see, there is a vast gulf between evangelism and advertising/sales. Sure, many of the tactics are similar and they share certain characteristics, but the similarity is superficial.

First, there is always a level of fanaticism involved in evangelism. High emotions mixed with dynamic personalities, topped off with just a shot of over-the-top showmanship, and you have an evangelist. Your typical evangelist can sing a good song, tap out a spiffy dance, but rarely is founded in consistent principles, logic, and reason. They almost always know the basic talking points, but have almost never delved deeper than the surface on any doctrine.

They seek the big emotional conversion. Shouting from the stage with the flash of fame, and the passing of the collection plate; they swoop their congregation off its feet and impart a miracle of the emotions that will hopefully last until the next performance, and the next passing of the collection plate. These people should be avoided, no matter how they make you feel.

The second problem, in regards to the evangelist, is his tendency to be a proselytizer. He tends to not be satisfied by simply helping those who are looking for directions, but he seems to want to rush out onto the highways of life and stop traffic so he can tell everyone the way to get to the location he thinks they should be heading towards. Typically the evangelist's flamboyance and showmanship are only overshadowed by his incredible assumption of self-importance. He doesn't just want to sell his goods, he wants everyone to want him. His primary product is himself, and his message is secondary at best, although usually the message comes in a distant third in importance after his stage performance. Again, we don't need these people. They are cheerleaders, having little understanding of, and no effect on the actual game.

One may ask; if we don't emphasize evangelical recruiting, how will our numbers ever grow to the point that we can have a real impact?

This question typically assumes two fallacies. The first and worst being the fallacy that we need a majority or we need vast numbers to "win". We don't. Democracy be Dammed! We will never have a majority, we shouldn't care about a majority, and we don't need a majority! Market thinking isn't about majorities; let the collectivists worry about majorities. We only need a better product, and we already have that. The second fallacy is the assumption that it's our job to recruit anarchists. It is not our job to recruit anarchists. Humans are born anarchists, it's our true nature. Tricks fool people into believing in the State, and as long as those people are comfortable in their pods clicking the feed bar, you will never be able to truly "convert" them to freedom. And again, we don't need to. The failings of the State do a far better job of waking up the anarchist spirit in people than any two bit/soap box/YouTube preacher ever has or ever could. Selling a product to those who are looking for that very product is vastly easier and more rewarding than evangelism.

We're talking about the difference between religious fanaticism and market demand. The word "evangelist" comes from the word "angel" and literally means; divinely sent messenger. Again, we don't need them.

Speaking of divinely sent messengers, the hard truth is that we don't need any Beloved Elderly Leader and former politician from Texas selling us more politics as a path to freedom any more than we need a Great Philosopher from Canada to enlighten us and indoctrinate us into his internet hate-your-mother cult. Politicians and cult leaders of any kind are worse than the cheerleading evangelists. If your version of "liberty" depends upon a weekly message from any Great Man, you are doing it wrong and this book is not aimed at you.

The State is the great recruiter of anarchists. Having an intellectually stimulating conversation with your fellow polo players at the country club on a Sunday afternoon, or the internet version of that scenario played out on social media, may create a theoretical anarchist. My experience has consistently shown that these theoretical anarchists get a big thrill out of changing their on-line profile to include an anarchist flag and adding some phrase to their header that includes the word "voluntaryism" or "agorism". But the moment there's a boots-on-the-ground test of these theoretical anarchists they'll start to puke statist blather like beer spewing from a freshman on frat pledge night. The reason for this phenomenon is complex, and unnecessary to evaluate here. For the purpose of this manual all we need to keep in mind is that the State does the job that rhetorical hoop jumping simply can't accomplish. Telling a person about the boot of the State may stimulate them intellectually. But when Officer Friendly actually drags their child out of a car and beats him half to death, the change of heart is real and permanent. Our job is to guide that change of heart, and encourage others to be empathetic. The State is its own worst enemy. It will kill itself. The question is; will we let it live long enough to take all of us out with it when it goes?

Right now you should be asking; short of having everyone's child sacrificed to the State to prove we're right about the State, what can we do?

(4.1.1) The Seven Part Job
The aboveground network's seven part job, in order of priority:
1. Provide for yourself and your family.

Dependence is the opposite of independence. The optimum situation is to secure an income stream that doesn't depend on the State. However, if providing for your family means a government job that doesn't require you to directly aggress upon the innocent, then you have to do what you have to do to survive. Not everyone has the luxury of an optimum situation, so first provide as best as you can.

2.   Strive for consistent principled behavior in your own life.

To steal a phrase; rather than focusing on the splinter in your neighbor's eye, you should make sure there's not a log in your own. If you believe what you say, you will live it. If you aren't living what you say, you don't believe it. Living a principled life is a reward of its own. You don't have to wait for some coming glory or some pie-in-the-sky. When you look in the mirror and you know the person looking back is genuine, and when you close your eyes at night knowing you have been true to yourself, you will live a happier life.

3.   Prepare for the systematic failure of the State. (beans, Band-Aids, Bitcoin, bullion, and bullets)

Survivalists and preppers have endured concentrated defamation by believers in the State. This fact alone means we should take note of their activities, because they're doing something that scares statists. That's not to say we should believe every foil-hat wearing wacky-doodle with a survival web site or podcast. We shouldn't. Some of them are seriously disjointed and some of them are pure con men running scams on the gullible. But being connected to the prepper community and being prepared for a variety of natural or man-made disasters is never a bad idea. Having a disaster plan, and having a Get-Out-Of-Dodge plan should be standard operating procedure. Also having a skill set that includes some survival and do-it-yourself abilities is never a bad thing. For example, every parent should know some basic first aid.

4.   Help those whom you can help and let-go of those whom you cannot help.

Emergency workers are trained in triage so that they may assign the priority of treatment based on the degree of injuries or illnesses of a large number of patients. For me, the most difficult part of triage is when you recognize the patient's condition is such that you cannot save them, and helping them will prevent you from helping someone else.

You don't want to walk away, but you can't stay. Some simply cannot be saved. That's not to say you must shun family or friends. It doesn't mean you should "de-foo" anyone. It means you must come to grips with the fact that some of them will never leave the mental comfort of slavery. They will cling to their chains to their last breath. Accept it and move on with your life. It's not your job to force slaves into freedom.

5. Expose the evil and lies of the State as you speak truth in the face of power.

One of the hardest things a person can do is to stand on the truth when the world around you is swimming in lies. One of the bravest things a person can do is to speak truth in the face of power. Some state this phrase as "speak truth to power" but as others have shown, that statement is flawed as it indicates that we should seek to change the minds of those in political power by influencing them with our words. We should not. Attempting to influence those who hold political power to do our will, morally places us in the same category as every other person who uses the political means to achieve their goals. Speaking truth in the face of power indicates that we are speaking in spite of the threat we face. We are not speaking to power, we are speaking truth to posterity, and the powers be damned!

6. Publicly disassociate yourself from the underground, denouncing all acts of aggression.

This requires a delicate balance. There are times when we can carefully take a lesson from our enemy. A myriad of politicians over the last few thousand years have turned double talk into an art form. By that I mean, answering a direct pointed question by talking around the topic while boldly announcing some ethical point that is very similar to the question but doesn't directly address the question. In doing this one can avoid telling a lie while avoiding the question. For example; if the topic of violent anarchists causes someone to accuse you of supporting violence you can explain the Zero Aggression Principle (or Non-Aggression Principle if you prefer that terminology) and you can further explain that some people who call themselves anarchists are actually communists and socialists and they do tend toward violence and destruction, since they don't respect property ownership. However peaceful anarchists embrace the Zero Aggression Principle (or NAP) so we reject all initiation of aggression, and we respect the property of peaceful people. When you take that path, deception may be employed and some say there is no difference between deception and a lie, but that is a matter for the individual to decide for their situation.

However, if you actually discipline yourself to avoid acts of aggression and commit yourself to peaceful means, this task of disassociation becomes much easier. But no matter the method, there must be a public disassociation between peaceful activism and the underground.

7.   Safely engage in direct activism.

Things like filming police, podcasting, or other activities, or quietly providing support for the underground, according to your abilities and resources. That "support" doesn't necessarily require money or direct contact. There are many things the individual may do to support the underground without directly interacting with those activists. Again, your imagination is a required tool in this endeavor. Or, if you have carefully examined yourself and you are one of the few uniquely suited for direct involvement in the underground movement, then pursue that path with care and wisdom.

(4.1.2) Film the Police While You Can

Filming police in America is an important form of activism right now but this situation is temporary. Governments worldwide, including the American government, have or will shut this window the moment they think they can get away with it. Currently there are several great organizations who are emphasizing the importance of filming the police, and they're training more and more people on how to safely do so. In America, these activists have given the State its most serious bloody nose of modern times. Right now the US government is stuck with old legal decisions and definitions that force it to not only allow the recording of police, but to actually protect those who are bold enough to do so. But as I said, that will rapidly change. Either courts will simply shift their legal protection away from those doing the filming, or what is more likely, some grand event will take place and the media and the full force of its propaganda wing will descend on the activists, demonizing them. In all likelihood this will be some kind of big tragic event somehow caused by someone filming police, and most likely it will involve the deaths of police or perhaps even children. Of course this event will be staged or if real, perhaps entirely orchestrated by the State for the purpose of shifting public opinion towards condemning those who film police.

An aspect of the "solution" to this terrible tragedy will be a federal level government emphasis on police forces filming themselves. Vast amounts of federal funding will assure a "solution" to this horrible event, maybe even a whole new department of federal employees will be hired to film the police for us. In reality, of course, government filming themselves only means more surveillance on the public and more police control of the actual recordings produced. Police will get better at producing fake videos, and the bulk of the public will buy the ruse without question.

The two action items here are: One; get as many activists filming police as possible while preparing those activists for the propaganda storm that will hit when the false flag event happens. Two; prepare for the time to come when it will be illegal to film police. The filming must continue after it becomes illegal, but it will need to take on a more clandestine approach.

If you just read that last paragraph and thought to yourself; "If we know a false flag event is coming and will likely be staged or orchestrated, why not just expose it as fake when it happens?" Fear not friend, there is already an army of activists waiting with baited breath for each new false flag event, so that they can be the one exposing its fraud. We are well represented in that field of battle. For more information just do an internet search for the phrase "crisis actor". However, the bulk of the public will believe the government lies no matter how poorly constructed and no matter how carefully debunked.

What about filming after the State forbids it? The black market exists only because the white market has become dangerous or forbidden. The same is true with activism. We can't allow laws and thuggery to determine our path. We must do what must be done.

(4-2) Fictional Beings and Their Property

Join me in a thought exercise.

The Setup: We understand that according to consistent libertarian philosophy every human has the exact same rights as every other human. So a child has the same right of property as an adult. Human's own themselves and have the right to own other property that they have rightfully come to possess.
We believe that two people may engage in a voluntary transaction, transferring the rightful ownership of property from one party to the other, and no one else may rightfully interfere. Libertarians also believe that unowned property can rightfully be homesteaded. This is not an exhaustive explanation of libertarian property theory, but it is suitable for this thought experiment.

Phase 1: With the above being the case, let us consider Sally, a child who owns a ball. Sally was given the ball by her mother Betty, who purchased the ball from a market. The ownership of the ball has not been in question up to the time that Sally decided to give the ball to her imaginary friend, Canada. Sally imagines Canada as an intelligent nine foot tall half-zebra-half-ape creature wearing a clown outfit. Sally deeply believes in Canada, believes she has relinquished ownership, and believes she no longer owns the ball. It's Canada's ball and Sally won't touch it.

Question 1: Can the fictional creature Canada, rightfully own the ball?

Phase 2: Every aspect of the above still remains except Sally is joined in her fiction by Billy, her real life neighbor who also believes in Canada.

Question 2: Does the union of Sally and Billy in their belief in the fictional being Canada, change the ownership of the ball?

Phase 3: Every aspect of the above still remains except that Sally's mother Betty, also believes in Canada.

Question 3: Does the authority of Betty, along with the union of Sally and Billy in their belief in the fictional being Canada, change the ownership of the ball?

Phase 4: This phase has a dramatic change. Sally's mother Betty stole the money she used to buy the ball. She is an outstanding pick-pocket, and over the course of a day of theft she stole money from seventy three people, totaling $418. Betty has no idea who those people were and it's impossible to find out who they were or return their share of the stolen money.

With that money Betty purchased groceries, gasoline, the ball for Sally, and she ate lunch at a restaurant, tipping the waiter generously. Upon leaving the restaurant Betty saw a homeless man picking through a trash can, so she gave the man $20. Every other aspect of the story remains the same. Sally gave the ball to Canada, while Billy and Betty both believe in Canada.

Question 4: Who owns the ball? Let me rephrase the question: Can a unrealistic fictional non-human entity own property purchased with untraceable stolen money, and does Betty's charity effect the question of property ownership?

If, at this point, you would argue that the fictional person Canada actually owns a ball, then our conversation would be over. I wouldn't bother attempting a debate someone who believes such outlandish fantasies. However, if you don't believe Canada can rightfully own property why would you believe an equally ridiculous unrealistic fictional non-human entity called the United States Government can own property?

...but wait! There's more!

Phase Crazy: Canada is no longer named Canada. Canada is now named General Energy. Sally, Billy and Betty believe they work for General Energy or GE as they call it. The US Government has issued a slip of paper that declares GE a legal "person". GE receives millions of dollars in stolen money (taxes) from the US Government every year in government contracts, and in return Sally Billy and Betty make guns that GE sells to the US Government. The US Government then uses those guns to collect the taxes that it pays to GE for more guns. Betty, using the legal authority granted by the US Government, uses GE's money to buy a ball for GE.

Question 5: Now who rightfully owns the ball?

The consistent libertarian should always have the same answer: The ball is unowned property. Anyone may rightfully homestead it and do with it as they please because imaginary fictional beings can't own property in the real world. This principle is not changed by the number of people believing the fiction, nor by the authority of the people believing the fiction, nor by their acts of charity.

And just because some old farts who call themselves "justices" or any other gang of delusional people with made up titles of glory, use enforcer-thugs to beat, cage, or kill anyone who disagrees, it doesn't change the reality of what is right and what is wrong. Nor is reality changed by the passage of time, so just because your father and his father before him believed in a nine foot tall half-zebra-half-ape named Canada, that doesn't make it so.

There are those who will attempt to argue that somehow the ball belongs to all of us. These people believe in "public property". They will use convoluted collectivist property rights theories to show that since we were all robbed then we all have ownership in the ball. To make this argument you must abandon libertarian principles and largely, logic itself. You have to create an imaginary world where you can theoretically own something without ever having seen it, touched it, or possibly even been aware of its existence. You would have to be able to own property that you can't possess or interact with in any way, and that you have no influence as to whether others may or may not interact with it. So then the question becomes; can you own a ball that you don't know exists and that someone else can play with or destroy at their will, while you have no say in its destiny? If you believe so, I wonder; do you also have a special friend named Canada?

At this point I should address the property of corporations that are not in a crony or codependent relationship with governments. Let us say an old man and an old woman have a little shoe sales/repair shop and have been running this humble business for years. Lately the neighborhood has changed, property values have skyrocketed, and their little niche business is expanding daily. They have had to hire employees, expand their shop, and have added a little tea shop in the building next door. For years they have been running their business as a simple "DBA", but now their accountant advises them that their business is at great risk if they don't form a corporation to protect it. Their actions to protect their business are morally very different from the actions of a corporation that is dependent upon its relationship with government.

If there is or if there is not a magic paper distinguishing the difference between the Mom-and-Pop shoe store and some corporation that is the exclusive shoe supplier to the prison-industrial-complex, there is still a moral difference. The old man and the old woman are reacting to the threat of theft by government or government assisted entities, whereas the other corporation is facilitating and profiting from that theft. Every moral anarchist should understand this difference in the same way that we understand that it is immoral to rob people to pay for roads, but it is not immoral to use that road once it is built. The difference being active robbery and a reaction to a robbery after the fact. To blame a victim for their reaction to a crime is shifting the responsibility away from the criminal and onto the victim.

If I have done my job here, then we can agree that property in the possession of fictional beings is rightfully unowned, in spite of the fact that there are people willing to kill on command for that fictional being. So rightfully, all State property (remember the definition of the State), including the property of governments, their crony churches, their crony corporations, the banking cartels, the main stream media, all of it, is unowned and rightfully open for homesteading. Once homesteaded, the new owner may rightfully do with it as he/she pleases, so long as he/she doesn't initiate aggression on the rightfully owned property of another real person. An example could be a window of a government vehicle. I could homestead it and immediately decide I wanted to break it. Rightfully, I could do so without violating libertarian property rights and without violating the zero aggression principle. However, the odds are the window is protected by a violent nut-job that believes in Canada and will shoot me down like a rabid dog, given the opportunity. Yes; he would be the aggressor and yes; I could rightfully protect myself, but remember, wisdom provides the balance between what I can rightfully do and what I should do.

Most freedom loving activists should not engage in violence in support of liberty, even justifiable violence. Most people are not very well endowed to deal with the physical and mental challenges, and the responsibilities that come with violence. However the wise activist who is naturally suited for violence but is still dedicated to the zero aggression principle, has a choice of the types of activism to be engaged in.

Simple sabotage is such a wide field of activism that the friend of freedom can carefully and safely choose the level and type of simple sabotage that best suits their individual situation. On the other hand, ethics-based irregular warfare requires a high level of self-discipline coupled with a very special skill set. Not every gun owner, for example, or former military, in spite of what they may think, is suited for the challenges of the early stages of irregular warfare. Near the end of the life of the State we may not have the luxury of choosing to be involved in war or not, but today while we can plan, and cities have not yet become glowing ashen craters, it is critical that the actions of the irregular warriors be wise, carefully planned, and be executed with extreme caution and secrecy.

More specific details on ethics-based irregular warfare and simple sabotage can be found in Sedition Subversion and Sabotage Field Manual No.1, in the section titled Ethics-Based Irregular Warfare and in the section titled Simple Sabotage.

(4-3) The Aboveground and The Underground

When the aboveground activist considers getting involved in the underground, an old saying applies; discretion is the greater part of valor. If you're not careful in whom you support and what activity you support you may be taking far more risk than you should. Consider the case of Samuel Mudd, the physician who set the broken leg of John Wilkes Booth. There were very loose connections between Booth and Mudd, and little to no connections between Mudd and the assassination of Abraham Lincoln, and yet in a frenzy to convict, a military court found Mudd guilty of aiding and conspiring in the murder, and he was sentenced to life imprisonment, escaping the death penalty by one vote.

Lori Fortier may have narrowly escaped a similar fate after the bombing of the Alfred P. Murrah Federal Building in downtown Oklahoma City on April 19, 1995. Apparently she helped Timothy McVeigh laminate a fake driver's license that he later used to secure the rental truck that carried a bomb on that faithful day. Any more involvement by Lori Fortier is based on conjecture at best. However, rather than see her railroaded through a kangaroo court and punished for something she had nothing to do with, her husband flipped and became a government stooge. Had he not done so she may have faced the same unreasonable guilt by association that Mudd had suffered.

The hard and ugly lesson being; supporting underground activists can be extremely dangerous. Know who you support and get some kind of idea as to their activities otherwise, if they fail or botch their get-away, you may suffer for crimes you had nothing to do with.

In the vast majority of situations, the aboveground activists should have no association with the activities of the underground, and at some time in the future even knowing who they are will be extremely dangerous. The best course of action will always be to disassociate yourself from the underground in every way. Publicly disavow them, and publicly renounce them. And never allow yourself to have financial connections with them as this will be an easy route the State will use to track down the underground and punish all involved.

(4-3.1) The Sabotage Pincer and The Aboveground Pincer

Hackers and friend-saboteurs should work to agitate the State by seeking out weaknesses in its security, transportation, manufacturing, and communication infrastructures, then exploiting those weaknesses, if possible, to cause systemic failure or at least confusion. At the point of systemic failure the hackers' and friend-saboteurs' work is done and the aboveground becomes the point of agitation by consistently advertising the failures of central planning and forced compliance, while trumpeting the advantages of spontaneous order and peaceful voluntaryism. This is the essence of the duel pincers of the scorpion. This type of agitation causes the State to overreact, and because of the nature of the State, that overreaction is always some kind of violent authoritarianism. As has been stated over and over, when you only own a hammer every problem looks like a nail, and with the State that means every problem becomes an opportunity for the State to pound someone. This violent overreaction by authoritarians presents the second opportunity for the aboveground activists to point out the evil nature of government, and again advertise the advantages of spontaneous order and peaceful voluntaryism. Therefore if done correctly, every successful action of the hackers and friend-saboteurs pays off twice for the aboveground in opportunities to bring shame on those who still support the State and in offering a moral solution.

This is the metaphor behind the term "Lego Distribution Network". The idea being that as soon as the State is asleep we slip in and spread Legos on the carpet. Then in the middle of the night when the State gets up to go to the bathroom, he will step on them. Hopefully he will stumble and fall down the stairs, but even if he doesn't fall, we will know that we are bringing him pain and aggravation.

The aboveground and the underground can also work separately to reveal as much information as possible about specific State supporters of aggression. This can involve public revelations of the inner workings of the so called "shadow governments" or "double governments" described by Michael Glennon and discussed later in this manual. These public revelations can include information about how double governments work, how politicians are actually powerless and are simply a show for the public, and how foreign and domestic policies are created to control the masses, not to keep them safe. In addition to this critical work, the aboveground and the underground can also work separately to reveal private and personal information about key figures in the double government so that the stinger of the scorpion can have the sufficient information that it needs to facilitate the decision making process when a stinging strike is required. The aboveground and the underground can be the eyes of the stinger.

Of course the obvious warning has to be inserted here. Whenever the State reacts to the above described agitation, activists of all kinds should be as far out of the reach of the State as possible. This is why invisibility and security are so critical to all components of the underground networks, and it's why the aboveground must have no direct ties to the underground. Consider the case of the journalist Barrett Brown who boldly and bravely supported the hacker collective, Anonymous, while writing news releases about their exploits and helping to build a wiki to facilitate analysis of their hactivism. Even though Barrett never did any hacking, when the US government and its crony cohorts at Stratfor suffered an embarrassing email leak in 2011, Barrett became a convenient whipping boy to be singled out and punished as an example for the rest of us.

Journalists like Brown, and others who have suffered even worse for their profession such as Michael Hastings and Gary Webb, walk a narrow tightrope balancing between their drive to expose the truth and the tendency to become part of the story, all the while standing in the open completely exposed to the slings and arrows of the State's fury. But for the rest of the aboveground, the best defense against being punished for the actions of the underground is to have no discoverable connections to the underground, and of course, a consistent public history of denouncing them won't hurt your case either.

(4-3.2) The Stinger: Natural Law, Defense, and Aggression

I am intentionally being vague in this section of this manual in reference to ethics based selective irregular warfare, as it is covered more completely and carefully in the section of this manual appropriately named "Ethics Based Selective Irregular Warfare". Among the reasons for being imprecise in this regards, in addition to the obvious reason of avoiding redundancies, is because at some point this manual may be physically divided into its three parts and those who need to read this section will have no need of being associated with those who have a need to read that section. In other words, it may be important for some activists to physically possess a copy of this section of the manual that doesn't contain the other two sections.

That said, by abandoning the trivium while embracing The Prussian Education System, western governments have systematically stymied the ability of many people to examine an ethical dilemma, break it down to its core questions, and develop a consistent logical solution. For that reason, a simple transitive equation such as the following, can confuse some people: If $A>B$ and $B>C$ then the equation $A>C$ can be assumed to be true without separate analysis. What one sees when interacting with many otherwise intelligent people is that they have, for example, adopted $A<C$ as dogma for a variety of reason, and simply cannot reexamine their position, despite the fact that they still agree that $A>B$ and $B>C$. This is often the source of the problem we face when attempting to explain questions of ethics using grammar, logic, and rhetoric, while contradicting tradition and authority. Many otherwise intelligent people simply cannot wrap their minds around concepts that are contradictive to what they have been taught.

To put that statement in beer gut terminology, no matter what your momma, your teachers, or some liberty Great Man told you, what I'm about to lay on you is Truth, so grab your socks before you get clipped in the neck.

There are laws throughout nature, waiting to be discovered on an as-needed basis. In and of themselves, they are neither good nor evil. Gravity, for example, is not good nor is it evil. It simply is. We wouldn't say that the man who falls to his death is a victim of evil gravity. That would be absurd. Yet when we see something that seems to defy natural law we quickly recognize that something is not quite right, and we tend to want to know why. We literally discover law through investigation and the resulting understanding of how things in nature work. This can be demonstrated by showing a simple slight-of-hand magic trick to a human child or even some other animals. A well-known internet video shows an orangutan viewing a magic trick. The ape is both amazed and humored. The reason he shows such interest in the trick is because he knows something has happened that seems to defy what he understands to be natural law, and his curiosity drives him to fascination with the phenomenon.

All animals have a certain built-in understanding of their role in nature and in the limits of nature. The same goes for the behavior of any animal. The lioness is not evil for providing her cubs with the flesh of a gazelle. She is simply following the law. Her behavior is required to preserve the lives of her offspring. If the gazelle had been able to escape the jaws of the lioness and the cubs had gone hungry, the gazelle would not be considered evil for starving the cubs. The lioness is following natural law, as is the gazelle when it seeks the opposite result of the encounter. In such an encounter natural law is not contradictive, it is beautifully consistent and a source of life and true peace. Evil, then, is what humans perceive when we see natural law violated in an unjust way by a human. Specifically when one human unjustly uses violence or threats of violence on another human, we know this is wrong the same way the orangutan knows something is not right about the magic trick. The difference being that at times, humans choose to violate natural law through unjustified violence, and this is why self-defense must enter the equation to fully understand the relationship of natural law and peace.

Since self-defense is a reaction to the breaking of natural law, not an original action in and of itself, it is exempt from law, and its execution is at the discretion of the person acting in self-defense. So for example, if Man A initiates violence on Man B by punching Man B in the nose, we may hope or expect Man B to retaliate by punching Man A back in return. However we may not see justification for Man B if he sprayed gasoline on Man A and set him on fire. Most people would perceive the fire as an overreaction. But do we have the natural right to make that judgment? Did we feel the pain, the fear, the trauma? Have we lived Man B's life? Do we know what it means to be Man B and to be attacked by Man A? This is the difference between natural law and civil behavior, and some have argued it is the basis of civil law. Natural law says that once Man A initiated the confrontation, the judgement of what is just punishment is rightfully in the hands of Man B, and he alone. Only Man B knows what it is like to be Man B and suffer that specific assault by Man A. Where civil behavior enters the equation is in the fact that the rest of us may or may not want to live around someone who would burn a man to death over a punch in the nose. So we rightfully may exclude Man B from association, but there is nothing in natural law that would condemn Man B for his chosen form of retaliation.

In the last five thousand years or so, judgments in civil behavior gave rise to agreements and eventually they became codes of acceptable civic behavior. Eventually limits were placed on both self-defense and retaliation and governments became the so-called authority of justice. In the case of Hammurabi's code for example, retaliation was unnaturally enforced by government at the arbitrary line of "eye for eye, tooth for tooth, bone for bone", and as all government programs tend to do, agreements in civil behavior became incredibly intrusive laws enforced at the point of a spear, controlling everything from contract law, to sexual forbiddances, to wage and price controls, and government began dictating punishments that depended upon the social ranking and wealth of the offender and the victim. All of this within the scope of Hammurabi's code. So what we see when we compare natural law with civil behavior is that natural law is never arbitrary, is fair, and always pushes us towards survival of our species, while civil behavior tends to be based on secondary observations by those who have no natural right to judge the matter, and tends to drift toward unfairness and intrusions based on social standing and wealth, where punishments are handed down from government officials.

In other words, civil rules of behavior and second party judgments must never supersede natural laws and primary party judgements, otherwise natural laws get replaced by government edicts and even the original civil rules become null and void as tyranny replaces freedom and justice become a commodity to be purchased at a government set price.

This leads us to consider self-defense and possibly discover an aspect of natural law. Remember the aggressive Man A and his violent attack on Man B? Is it possible that Man B's overreaction to the punch in the nose could have been avoided had he spotted the threat Man A presented and acted in preemptive self-defense? If Man B had recognized Man A's intent to punch, and once there was no doubt the event was imminent, if Man B had struck first, would Man B not have been more evenly tempered to judge the follow-through retaliation against his attacker, having not been subjected to the disorienting effects of the nose punch? In other words, perhaps if Man B had acted in preemptive self-defense there would be no need for the naysayers to wag their fingers in civil judgement of his actions because he very likely never would have set Man A on fire. In all likelihood the event would have ended with Man A being taught a quick lesson by way of a few bruises, and with Man B avoiding humiliation, pain, and the judgment of his peers. Natural law drives the species toward survival, as both men come out better for the encounter. Thus we see that preemptive violence can be an act of self-defense, and is consistent with natural law. If, on the other hand, Man A simply can't learn this lesson, perhaps we are all better off without him in the gene pool. But that is not for us to judge, it is for his next victim to decide.

This leads to our next step in discovering natural law, in regards to self-defense. If you have knowledge that a man is stalking your child with the intent to harm her, you are following natural law when you interrupt that man's aggression before he harms your child. And if that man has a history of murdering innocent children, you are under no moral obligation to spare his life in the defense of your child, before he has a chance to act. In a situation such as this, preemptive defense is not only wise, but within the natural law definition of ethical action.

Many adherents to the Zero Aggression Principle attempt to argue that we may not defend ourselves until after the physical aggression has been initiated by the attacker. This is illogical for several reasons, the first of which is that true defense, by its nature, involves the presentation to the potential attacker the prospect that an attack will have a price, so that the attacker can choose to avoid the confrontation to begin with. Otherwise we could be considered baiting the attacker if the attacker has the impression that he may have the first strike "free". Remember, almost every dangerous or poisonous animal in nature has clear markings to warn its attackers. After all, in many situations the attacker who has his first shot free often leaves the victim incapable of self-defense after that first strike. For example, I am about 6 feet tall and weigh around 240 pounds; additionally I have trained in personal combat including the European martial art of pugilism. If I, or someone of comparable size and skill, were to get a totally free bare knuckle first punch in a fight, the fight would likely be instantly over, no matter the size, strength, or training of the victim. That is clearly not a natural law situation that advances our species or promotes peace. So then, natural law provides for preemptive self-defense while remaining within the constraints of the Zero Aggression Principle.

Now consider the following: According to the FBI, in 2014 burglary losses in the US topped out at $3.5 billion. In that same year, according to the Institute For Justice, US "law enforcement" stole $4.5 billion using asset forfeiture laws. Don't be confused by such a huge number by thinking that massive amounts of money was taken from big time drug dealers, because that didn't happen. The median forfeiture amount in 2014 was less than $500. Now ask yourself how you would treat a known burglar? If half of all burglars wore distinctive uniforms with a clearly displayed badge indicating they are a burglar, how would you treat them? Would they be safe walking down your street? Would they be safe sitting in a clearly marked car in your neighborhood? Now consider that there were roughly 20,000 no-knock raids in the US in 2014, and that number is rising every year. The largest crime gang in the world already wear uniforms, carry military grade weapons, and steal more from peaceful people than all of their competitors combined, and that doesn't count what is stolen in taxes and through inflation.

The above being the case, if we have clearly demonstrated that a specific institution is based on intimidation, violence, and theft, and if we have demonstrated that specific employees or representatives of that institution have a proven record of using intimidation, violence, and theft to advance that institution and themselves, and if we have demonstrated that said representatives of said institution are both willing, capable, and at some point in the future, likely to repeat such aggressions upon ourselves, our loved ones, or other equally innocent victims, then we are not under obligation to wait until that specific aggressor strikes the first blow against us or our families. And if both the institution and the representative of that institution are known to kill the innocent, we have no obligation to limit our use of force when defending ourselves and family from that aggressor. Actually, much like the lioness above, it is our natural responsibility to preserve our family and remove threats before they can do harm, and like the law of gravity, the natural law of defense cannot be logically described as evil. It simply is.

Back to beer gut terminology, they are in our towns, they are in our neighborhoods, and they are daily entering our homes and having their way with our property and our loved ones. They don't think we can or will do a thing about it. But they are wrong. We can and we will stop them. But we must do it wisely! We cannot foolishly play into their hands through open confrontation.

5. TECHNOLOGY, HACKING, AND SECURE COMMUNICATIONS

One of the most obvious shortcomings of this manual will be the lack of specifics in the fields of technology and hacking. The reason is that the hacking world moves and changes so fast that a manual such as this would be outdated to the point of laughter before I could consult the right people, translate from hackerese to American English, and publish it.

Also, to a large extent, the hacker community has a far better grasp of most of the concepts outlined in this manual, since they have been in the fields fighting the good fight, taking serious risks, while the bulk of the "liberty movement" were either engaged in arguments on social media or waving signs at a 420 rally. Not to say social media and 420 rallies are bad, they just don't compare to being sentenced to three life sentences in a federal penitentiary for running a forum, or being murdered and having it staged like a suicide because of a few lines of code. This is the reason that this manual is of the least value to the technology/hacking activists, however I will touch on a few items.

Operations security or OPSEC, is a science in and of its own. I am neither qualified nor motivated to devote 500 pages to the topic. One partial reason is that by 2009, as I investigated internet OPSEC, I became convinced that the typical internet-culture version of OPSEC was pretty much a faith based fantasy. If you hold "radical" political beliefs someone in a government office likely knows about it. They read or copy pretty much everything. Even if they aren't currently watching you and your specific activities, because they keep a record of almost everything, they can retroactively find out almost anything they want to know about you. A case in point is Ross Ulbricht, the alleged Dread Pirate Roberts. With an incredibly weak case against him, government investigators searched old entries at internet locations like the Mises Institute, to build a dossier based on user names similar to his and writing styles like his to determine an IP profile. Using weak connections like that, they focused in on Ross and warped the actual evidence in the case to convince a dim-witted jury that he was the devil incarnate. It didn't really matter if Ross was innocent, guilty, or anywhere between. He was their target and they were going to catch him and make an example of him simply because slave masters love to beat the whipping-boy, and Ross was a textbook whipping-boy.

Now consider the case of Matt DeHart, former U.S. Air National Guard intelligence analyst allegedly involved in an attempt to expose the CIA's involvement in the 2001 anthrax scare. Without enough actual evidence to convict Matt, authorities chose to seize his computers and plant images resulting in child pornography charges.

One may ask why so much time and effort was invested into the Ulbricht case when they could have just faked the evidence like they did in the DeHart case. The obvious answer is hidden in the fact that government agents working on the Dread Pirate Roberts case have been proven guilty of absconding with a fortune in Bitcoin that they stole from The Silk Road, and no such source of funding was available in the DeHart case. So they took the easy, time tested route of planting evidence on computer hard drives that the government had complete access to with no way to prove it wasn't Matt's pornography. So does that mean we should just throw caution to the wind and forget about internet security and private communications? Not at all. It means those in the underground should not worry about or try to be totally invisible, but we should learn and practice communicating in ways that assure the best security that is possible for the things that matter. One thing that helps us do that is if the aboveground activists practice secure communications for things that don't need to be private, if for no other reason, to keep the watchers busy watching things that don't matter.

(5-1) Secure Communications

As covered above in regards to activist networks, communication systems can be centralized, decentralized, or distributed in structure. An example of a currently working (2016) distributed communication system that provides good functionality, but doesn't rely on any centralized host is Tox (https://tox.chat/), it allows private chat, group chat, and file sharing, and is encrypted end to end (although the PC itself can still be compromised). It's a direct replacement for unsecured chat and secured chat that is centrally hosted. Currently the download and use are free of charge.

Another distributed project which is way more comprehensive towards secure communications and file sharing is RetroShare (https://en.wikipedia.org/wiki/RetroShare), and is more like a private bulletin board system, where you can post files and messages for others to download later. Neither of these two are very hard to set up, but they do both require the participants to somehow exchange their keys (preferably in a secure way) in order to connect to each-other.

Coupling either of the two distributed systems above with an operating system like Tails which gives out-of-the-box anonymity over Tor (review here: https://zomiaofflinegames.com/tails-2-0-is-here-download-now/), can give us a private secure network like we've never seen before, and it's not too hard to set up.

There are other systems like this coming out all the time, making the idea of putting such a topic in print seem rather silly.

6. HOMEWORK AND CONCLUSION

Homework Assignment A:

Assuming you have made it this far and completed this first section of this manual, I would like to assign some reading before you continue to the next section. The reason for this homework is to drive home the concept that the thing the public sees as "government" is not the State, and indeed, it is not even government. The political process with all its politicians, its posturing, its political campaigns, its elections, and all of its quasi-religious ceremonies is in fact an elaborate opera played out by actors for your entertainment. The entire show is nothing more than an on-going intravenous drip of political opiates to keep the public in a stupor. Actual government policies are the result of a hidden government made up of unelected semi-permanent bureaucrats who kindly play along with the politicians, while doing almost all of the work of running the apparatus of government. If you complete this homework assignment you will find the above statement is not a wild-eyed foil hat conspiracy. It is simply how the real world of government works, and if you complete this assignment, you will see a major flaw in the very fabric of government that is just waiting for someone to yank the thread and unravel the whole cloth.

The assignment; Read, or at least skim, the short book: "National Security and Double Government", by Michael Glennon (2014)

Michael Glennon is professor of international law at The Fletcher School of Law and Diplomacy at Tufts University. He is a respected Washington DC policymaker and insider. He is not an anarchist, he is not a conspiracy wacko, and he is not a whistleblower with an ax to grind. He is a solid statist who is being brutally honest with his collogues in describing a flaw that he perceives in American government.

Although insightful in regards to the national security/intelligence state, and revealing in his indictment of the process of selecting US Supreme Court justices and US presidents, Michael Glennon seems to ignore or not be aware of the struggle between the hidden government that he talks about, and the public government in the post WWII years, culminating in the assignation of a sitting US President. Perhaps he didn't want to muddy the waters with the topic, but ignoring such an event in conjunction with his lacking in assessment of the obvious meddling by the Central Banks and their owners in regards to monetary policy, and the massive influence of the military industrial complex, the pharmaceutical complex, the energy complex, and the industrial farming interests have all played, is disturbing to say the least. Again, perhaps there were constraints in time or perhaps he chose to only focus on the national security/intelligence issues because of his target audience or perhaps because he wished to keep the discussion in his realm of excellence. For whatever his reason, and considering the precision in his assessment, it is sad that he didn't follow through to a better conclusion than to just say that voters should be better educated. This failure stands out most dramatically when you consider that he never even once hints at the incredible level of aggression and violence that his so called "Trumanites" have relied upon to gain and maintain their grip on government. Also when you consider that the very system of "Trumanites" that he describes existed in American history before the date he points to as their official birth, and in fact controlled major aspects of the American government long before Harry Truman was born, his warnings seem far too little far to late. And again, to assume more education could be the solution considering the American education system was one of the first targets of the hidden government in the late 1800s, seems like a weak conclusion at best.

More to the interests of readers of this manual is the glaring weaknesses inherent in the American government that Glennon so carefully and accurately points out. From his article:

"The aim of this Article thus far has been to explain the continuity in U.S. national security policy. An all-too-plausible answer, this Article has suggested, lies in Bagehot's concept of double government. Bagehot believed that double government could survive only so long as the general public remains sufficiently credulous to accept the superficial appearance of accountability, and only so long as the concealed and public elements of the government are able to mask their duality and thereby sustain public deference. As evidence of duality becomes plainer and public skepticism grows, however, Bagehot believed that the cone of governance will be 'balanced on its point'. If 'you push it ever so little, it will depart farther and farther from its position and fall to earth.'"

Restating Walter Bagehot, Glennon lays out for us what we should already know; modern Western style government is entirely based on the lie that visible politics run governments when actually the hidden-in-plain-sight truth is that visible politics play almost no role in the actual policies of government, and the most important point of both Bagehot and Glennon being that the whole house of cards is at risk of collapse if the public fully figures it out. That leads us to the point of this manual; how to capitalize on that wonderful weakness and shove the "cone of governance" off of its balance point so that we may all shout with glee as Humpty Dumpty tumbles to the earth.

Homework Assignment B:

Think of ways you can assist the underground without being directly connected to the underground. Here's some examples, but see if you can think of more.

1. Do you know or have an interest in lock picking? This would be a great skill set to learn and teach to those in the underground.
2. Are you an actor or are you talented in that art? Could you develop acting troupes that could use their talent in the underground? You could practice at liberty functions and get-togethers by fooling the participants into thinking you were building inspectors, FBI agents, or worse. Aboveground activists with experience in specific fields can work as advisors as in; how do corrections officers behave, how do Federal Marshals transport prisoners, how do police talk to each other when no one is listening? For example, the movie "Burn After Reading" lost my attention when the great character actor J.K.

Simmons played the unnamed "CIA Superior" and began to talk. The few CIA operators I have known were nothing like that. The CIA agents I have encountered used very clean language, they were Mormons, and they were very dedicated and straight laced, all business all the time. In my experience, as good of an actor as J.K. Simmons is, I wouldn't believe for a moment that he was an actual CIA agent. Under the right circumstances, a mistake like that could cost an activist dearly.

3. Medical personnel, specifically those with trauma and emergency room experience, can hold classes teaching emergency first aid to members of the underground.

4. Organize an ambassador system with other anarchist and activist groups to provide them services during demonstrations/riots and other times. Perhaps film crews, news coverage, medical assistance, logistics, communications, alerts about police movements, or other services could be offered without getting directly involved in their causes or their demonstrations. NOTE ON OTHER GROUPS: Do not repeat the mistake Rothbard made with the Racist-Right! Infiltrate them, but do not water down our movement by evangelizing them! Do not trust them. Invade their circles, but do not let them in ours!

5. Train rescue teams before demonstrations/riots so that teams can rush in and remove injured protesters before they can be arrested. (possibly even after they are arrested) Training teams for spotting agents provocateur, identifying "Shadow Teams", and even shadowing the Shadow Teams while communicating their movements could be very important. Identifying Arrest Teams and communicating Arrest Team movements before they act, and even possibly training teams to disrupt the Arrest Teams, could be invaluable.

6. The greatest tool for liberty is your mind. Open it, take it out, and play with it. Remember, each of us has our own mind, but the State does not own such a tool.

Conclusion

On the physical and economic levels, the State is an inherently unstable parasitic collaborative of politicians/bureaucrats and select corporations, along with a subservient media, clergy, and intelligentsia, that relies upon a combination of extortion, intimidation, threats, and violence to dominate its human host. In doing so it distorts markets, stifles competition, discourages innovation, and through manipulation of the money supply and debt, siphons the lion's share of wealth into the pockets of a tiny group of central banking families, while destroying a good portion of the wealth that it doesn't steal. On a metaphysical level, the State, whether real or imagined, is a faith based deity existing in the minds of its believers, generally based on a combination of the adoration of a Great Man along with an illogical fear of a Bogeyman in conjunction with an unblinking faith in the political process. That faith in turn relies on a dramatic opera-like performance on the part of politicians as they attempt to appear relevant, while the shadow government of bureaucrats and corporate/banking puppet masters attempts to remain unseen. All the while the State struggles to provide services it claims the monopolistic right to provide, while miserably failing at providing those services. On the occasion that the State's true nature is revealed and its failures exposed, it always responds by sending in waves of lies by actors on all levels, while systematically discrediting, beating down, or murdering anyone who shines the light on those failures.

The State relies on an incredibly delicate balancing act between the disinterest of its victims, the imagery of a functioning political process, and faith in government-lead progress toward some mythical idea of a better tomorrow, in contrast with the reality of a non-functional puppet political process and an ever growing ever consuming Beast, driving humanity toward world-wide slavery at best, and species wide destruction as a very real possibility. In the past there have been four basic strategies for defeating the State, none of which actually provide a mechanism for defeating the State, while two of those strategies are either non-productive or, more commonly, destructive and counterproductive to our cause.

This manual proposes a fifth strategy based on the idea that it is possible to upset that balance by simply waking up both the disinterested and the faithful public. This is accomplished by prodding the powers that be into over-reactions, while boldly proclaiming the failures and lies of the current system. This manual posits that this process is inherently dangerous as the State, having its basis in violence and hate, will react using extreme measures. Further, this manual posits that the primary members and leaders of the State will react in varying levels of panic and desperation as their positions of power become more and more unstable. Finally this manual posits that in self-defense, specific activists will of necessity, be required to take actions that none of us would like to think about. In self-defense, those actions will be violent, bloody, and will encompass the power structure of the State and its supporting apparatus.

Concluding, this manual is a first attempt to motivate and train those brave activists who will accomplish this three-part task. This manual is not exhaustive, nor complete. It is in need of revision and modification by those who are committed to this fight and knowledgeable of the processes herein outlined.

END Part 1 PEACEFUL SEDITION

Part 2 SIMPLE SABOTAGE

A Note From The Director:
March 2016

This manual is published for the information and guidance of all our friends and should be used as the basic doctrine for sedition and subversion training in preparation for active simple sabotage, as a precursor to the ethics-based selective irregular warfare that will act as the final blow to the State. (See: Sedition Subversion and Sabotage Field Manual No. 1; Ethics Based Irregular Warfare) Sedition is defined as conduct or speech inciting the rejection of established authority. Subversion implies the use of economic, underhanded, covert, or violent methods to change or abolish governments. We acknowledge that the primary mission of anarchists should be to use peaceful methods of persuasion and propaganda to educate as many people as possible as to the evils of the State, and to use the positive aspects of sound economics and peaceful voluntary exchange to offer an alternative to aggression and war. We acknowledge that the vast majority of anarchists should not be involved in any violent or destructive behavior, and should quickly disavow any connection to violence and destruction. But we acknowledge that self-defense sometimes requires proactive measures. We also understand that foolish actions, however morally justified, will in all likelihood not result in a positive outcome. Therefore we submit this manual in an attempt to provide direction for those who are suited for taking the hard actions that others should wisely forgo.

PRECAUTIONS:

Generally speaking, sabotage instructions and subversive plans of all kinds should be dispersed in separate pamphlets or leaflets according to categories of operations and should be distributed with care and not broadly. They should be used as a basis for podcasts, internet articles, and low power radio broadcasts (only for local and special cases, best directed by your local committees of friends). As a collection, such instructions should be kept on secure drives with safe encryption.

PERSPECTIVE:

Going back into antiquity, various generations have repeated a version of the same myth; that being the idea that you are the chosen generation, and you are the children of destiny. This is the dawning of a new age, or of the end of ages. The Age of Aquarius has arrived. These are the "end times" or Jesus is about to return and we will be the generation who will see him returning in the clouds. This myth is not new, and it is not unique to this or any generation. One current manifestation of this myth has gained some popularity of late, that being the idea that we can have "liberty in our lifetime" or escape to a "Galt's Gulch" where we all live in peace. Most of the salesmen for these gimmicks are simply honest believers filled with hope serving the existing myth, but some are true con men who use these myths to milk the gullible of money or convince their followers to join some cult or movement. Usually a dynamic leader with an outlandish personality will convince the followers to send him their cash or to migrate to some remote location. Often once the big event fails to happen the movement either dies or mutates into a mainstream shadow of its former self. There are a variety of causes behind this repeating myth and the outcome can be tragic or benign or anywhere between. But the point is to recognize such myths for what they are and guard yourself from being caught up in this false hope.

Our enemy, the State, is in this for the long haul. He is not attached to one government, one central banking institution, one corporation, one royal family, or one generation. The State is a deity that is older than any other organized religion. Before Vasudeva beheld Krishna, the State was old. Before Buddha contemplated the meaning of peace, the State had perfected war. Before Father Abraham was born, the State had risen, fallen, and had risen again. The State was already ancient when an Egyptian pharaoh, for the very first time, bowed his knee and lifted a sacrifice to The Great Ra rising in the east. To understand the nature of the State, and then to believe that you are the one magic generation that will defeat this Beast is the height of arrogance.

The State feels no fear of us, and its current politicians, bureaucrats, central bankers, CEOs, police, and military industrial complex have no fear of us. Few of them even know we exist. And thus we have the advantage.

Without our enemy's knowledge we can fully infiltrate its structure. We can know what our captors are saying behind closed doors. We can plot the downfall of this deity from within the walls of its temples. But we cannot act with urgency. We must embrace wisdom and forgo dynamic personalities and the giant egos that drive wanna-be leaders. We must prepare for a generational battle. We must understand the weaknesses of collectivism and central planning, and develop the power of the individual independent scholar warrior. We must incorporate decentralization and distributed networks in our methods and teach the next generation how to take up this fight and continue it without depending on outlandish personalities and short-sighted gimmicks. We must take on the challenge that our forefathers sidestepped.

Yes! The State can be defeated in one generation! But it will most likely take us many generations of hard work to prepare that generation for its task. Thus far, most of the work done by anarchists has been confined to talking and arguing while repeating the same mistakes earlier anarchists have repeated since the time of their fathers. Now we must mature in wisdom and start developing the long battle. It's time for us to set aside the expectation of a Great Man to deliver us. It's time to ignore the cute cheerleaders (of all genders) on the sidelines and realize there is a hard and bloody task ahead and not everyone is fit for it. Not every step is a step in the right direction, and if we are going to reach the destination we seek we must plot out that path and stop running after every melodic voice that we hear in the wind.

Finally, this field manual is not a step by step literal guide. It is an outline of concepts. It is intended to stimulate thought. Some suggestions contained herein will be more valuable than others. Some suggestions will quickly become outdated. That is the reason this manual is listed as provisional, because it is not set in stone. The greatest weapon a human being owns is his own mind, and that is a weapon the State lacks. We expect you will use yours.

Grigori Rasputin V, Director
Committee of Friends,
Office of Sedition Subversion and Sabotage
Lego Distribution Network
Yefimovich, Pokrovskoye, Free Oblast

1. INTRODUCTION TO THE BASIC CONCEPTS OF SIMPLE SABOTAGE

(1-1) Why?

The purpose of this manual is to justify and characterize simple sabotage, to outline its possible effects, and to present suggestions for inciting and executing it to its fullest. We understand that the concept of the State is a mental construct based on the existence of coercive monopolistic governments in conjunction with key co-dependent corporations and others, used to control, manipulate, and enslave humanity. We understand that this system of coercive monopoly is nothing more than the current manifestation of the most successful crime gangs working in conjunction to extort the maximum amount of wealth from the residents of their respective agreed upon geographic territories. Further, we understand that coercive central planned governments are inheritably flawed, both morally and economically, and are thusly unstable. Left to themselves, violent governments tend to collapse, but in their fall they are typically replaced by an equally unstable and corrupt crime gang that become the new government, often made up of the most violent elements of the previous government. Therefore it is not the purpose of this manual to hasten the fall of one government so that it can be replaced by another. Rather, it is our goal to destabilize the concept of the State in the minds of its believers around the world so that we may all escape this cycle of coercion and slavery. To accomplish this goal, we are encouraging acts of sabotage as a method of exposing the instability and the failures of all governments to provide the services that they claim the monopolistic right to control.

A common fallacy that has worked to pacify one generation after the next is the idea that "capitalism" is the true evil and "inequality" is the enemy of humanity. (That's right, ambiguous words are our enemy.) In this scenario the faithful believer mostly ignores the concept of the coercive State and is convinced that with enough central planning by just the right people or some "Great Man", benevolent government can redistribute wealth and everyone will "get a piece of the pie".

In fact this silly notion ignores the hard facts of economics and is founded on an amazing ignorance of history coupled with a childish lack of morals. The fantasy that perfect central planning will produce equality, and that will in turn produce the perfect man who will be thrilled to live his life sweating in a communal factory or standing in line for bread, has instead always produced crushing poverty and starvation, followed by mass death and eventual government upheaval or revolution. Then finally, the adoption of the very type of "capitalism" that was hated to begin with. (This "capitalism" actually being fascism, in economic terms.)

Another common fallacy that has hindered many organized movements toward freedom is the myth that to shrink government or government's influence to a "manageable" size, would somehow weaken government and make the slavery of the coercive State acceptable. A segment of each generation believes that if they can wrestle control of government, perhaps through secession or through infiltration of government by "patriots" or some "Great Man"(usually a politician, celebrity, or military "hero"), then the nature of human beings will magically shift and coercion on a smaller local level will produce lasting peace and freedom. In other words the beatings will continue until morale improves. Of course this never happens. Coercion only produces more coercion. Theft doesn't stimulate productivity; it stimulates poverty and more theft. Prisons don't produce obedient docile citizens, they produce harder criminals. Rape doesn't stimulate love and affection; it creates hate and retribution. Small weak tyrants provide the opportunity for larger stronger tyrants. Much like revolution, secession and conservative policies simply lead to a change of guards on the prison walls with more violent deadly tyrants heading up local serfdoms that eventually become absorbed or annexed back into a developing empire, and the cycle repeats. The "conservative" dreams of a mythical past when government was "good", but in fact that history is a lie that never happened. Government was never good, and the "founding fathers" of today's conservatives were the progressive tyrants of yesterday's conservatives. In the end, both of these paths are simply the socialist veil of lies and tricks behind which the State has hidden throughout its bloody reign of terror. Misdirected belief in these myths has shown consistently to be the very foundations on which the perpetuation of the State rests.

Say not, "Why were the former days better than these?" For it is not from wisdom that you ask.
Ecclesiastes 7:10

In addition to everything stated above, history displays for us a predictable cycle that must be broken if humanity is ever to achieve freedom, or in fact even survive as a species. It is the nature of humans to suffer inconvenience and oppression rather than risk drastic and dangerous change, right up to the point that they can no longer tolerate the oppression. When they are frustrated to the point of uprising, typically some government actor, commonly an orator or military leader, will rise up to speak for the downtrodden. Violent action is taken and government either falls into bloody revolution, mass murder and war, then into the hands of a worse tyrant than before; or it appears to take on a dramatic metamorphic transformation into a manageable more tolerable "friendly" government based on promises or guarantees of "rights". It seems to the short term observer that this later development is good. In fact it is far worse than the open tyrant. Because of the economic advantages of the "friendly" government, business flourishes and the "friendly" government develops vast wealth and power that the openly tyrannical government could never have achieved. With this wealth the "friendly" government either develops an aggressive military culture or it becomes subservient to a government with an aggressive military culture. Which then turns its oppression outside its borders and becomes a far more deadly force than the openly tyrannical government could ever have achieved. With fanatical followers within its own borders, a radical military culture, and a more "business friendly" environment (corporate/government marriage), the "friendly" government becomes a far worse tyranny than it ever could have before it merged with business. Governments like this have become a force for evil that not only threatens humanity, but has now in our lifetimes become a threat to all life on the entire planet. At this point in time it's unclear how many more cycles of "good government" our species can tolerate. As odd as it may seem, wishing and working for a smaller more manageable government not only pushes the responsibility and burden to the next generation, it makes it more likely that new version of the "friendly" government will become something the last generation could not have imagined. This is how the cycle of "good government" works.

If we can come to the conclusion that we must stop doing the same thing over and over attempting to come up with a different result, then logic drives us to the old question; What shall this man do? The answer to that question is that we must learn the true art of war and incorporate wisdom into our efforts. Recognizing the above described cycle is one aspect of the principle of knowing one's self and knowing one's enemy. We must fight in a way that disarms our enemy while strengthening ourselves. We must stop believing that using the tools governments supply to us will work to defeat the State. We must reject all political solutions. We must reject civil disobedience, and every other method of begging the master for mercy. We must learn the weaknesses of central planning and collectivism, and develop the strengths of independence and individuality. We must reject the idea of tearing down the military industrial/banking complex and we must concentrate on learning how to cause the Beast to lose its footing and allow its own bloated torso to crush the thin legs that hold it up. For one practical example, we must stop silly pursuits like demanding government "End The Fed" and realize that we have the power to ignore the Fed through cryptocurrencies. Let governments run their debts to the sky and devalue their money. It only helps us in the long term as it proves our point, that governments are nothing more than criminal gangs and the State is a destructive religion that needs to pass into the dust heap of history with other nonsensical violent religions.

In knowing ourselves and knowing our enemy, we must recognize the vast resource advantages that the State possesses, and we must resist every traditional military action. Knowing that the State possesses an endless supply of young foolish men who will fight and die on command, while our numbers will always be limited to a small dedicated force, we can never fight the State using numbers, attrition, or open conflict.

Considering that our enemy possesses most of the world's wealth along with the ability to create more money on demand, it would be foolish to believe we can spend our way to victory.

When fighting a vastly more powerful opponent, the wise warrior simply doesn't allow his enemy to know where or who he is. We must never openly confront the State and reveal our positions, our strength, nor our intentions. Martyrs, messiahs, heroes and Great Men will not deliver us from this evil. Brave last stands, angry marches, civil disobedience, and loud proclamations will never serve our ends. Risking our numbers to occupy a physical location or region will only serve to make it easier for our enemy to find and subdue us. Openly petitioning and begging government has never and will never be the path to freedom. Openly threatening a vastly superior enemy is never wise. Our deliverance will come from an extended series of principled actions done clandestinely by individuals, based on wisdom and not emotion nor hero glorification. We must choose every battlefield and we must choose the timing and circumstances of every interaction. We must seek out our enemy's weak points and capitalize on them. We must systematically bring this Beast to its knees by its own weight. This is the role of simple sabotage, until such a time comes that our enemy is weakened to the point that the individual riflemen can finish the job by decapitation of the Beast through ethics-based selective irregular warfare. In this way simple sabotage is the precursor that will allow selective irregular warfare to be the final death blow to the State.

(1-2) What?

Sabotage varies from highly technical coup de main acts that require detailed planning and the use of specially-trained operatives, to innumerable simple acts which the ordinary individual friend-saboteur

can perform. This manual is primarily concerned with the latter type. Simple sabotage should not require specially prepared tools or equipment; it is executed by an ordinary friend of freedom who may or may not act individually and without the necessity for an active connection with an organized group; and it is carried out in such a way as to involve a minimum danger of injury, detection, or reprisal.

Where destruction is involved, the weapons of the friend-saboteur are such things as salt, nails, candles, pebbles, thread, lip balm or any other materials he might normally be expected to possess at home or as a worker in his particular occupation. His arsenal is the kitchen shelf, the trash pile, and his own usual kit of tools and supplies. The targets of his sabotage are usually objects to which he has normal and inconspicuous access in everyday life, and ideally, that others have access to as well.

A second type of simple sabotage requires no destructive tools whatsoever and only produces physical damage, if any, by highly indirect means. It is based on universal opportunities to make faulty decisions, to adopt a non-cooperative attitude, and to induce others to follow suit. Making a faulty decision may be simply a matter of placing tools in one spot instead of another. A non-cooperative attitude may involve nothing more than creating an unpleasant situation among one's fellow workers, engaging in bickering, or displaying surliness and stupidity. Introducing strife and division among fellow government employees, or playing up the weaknesses of management or recognized leaders. Even the spreading of rumors can be an effective form of sedition. In short, slacktivism (defined thusly) can be as effective if not more effective as traditional activism.

Slacktivism, sometimes referred to as the "human element," is frequently responsible for accidents, delays, and general obstruction even under normal conditions. The potential saboteur should discover what types of faulty decisions in the operations are normally found in his kind of work and should then devise his sabotage so as to enlarge that "margin for error" as far as reasonably possible without risking discovery. It's difficult to over-sell this point. One of, if not the major weakness of every government and every large corporation is the human element. The vast majority of government and corporate employees simply don't care if their employer runs efficiently and competitively or not. There is little to no motivation for the average employee to produce anything over the bare minimum, much less to excel above or beyond the mediocre level his fellow employees routinely produce. Thus we have the perfect environment to take the built-in errors of the human element and magnify them to the point of crippling the workings of governments and the key corporations that keep governments functioning.

Another example of simple sabotage using the human element can involve blackmail, extortion, and scandal. These types of operations can be quite dangerous and should be left to those experienced in such matters. However this type of simple sabotage can also be invaluable in both financing further operations, and in unveiling the despicable nature of the authoritarians.

For this reason training for such activities should be encouraged. Acting classes, practical demonstrations, step-by-step instructions, and the study of historical examples should be encouraged until teams are developed who can perfect this racket. Computer hackers are exceptionally effective in revealing personal information about politicians and other State actors. Famous main stream media personalities are often portrayed as honest and dependable but behind the scenes they are violent despicable thugs. Exposing them as such can be dangerous but extremely effective and rewarding. Also various forms of doxing can be extremely effective in harassing and demoralizing the leadership of the military industrial complex and the central banking complex. The wildly inappropriate reaction of government to the hacking in the Stratfor scandal show how much the powers-that-be fear the hacking community. And for good reason.

(1-3) Where?

Acts of simple sabotage should be occurring everywhere that our friends are located. Efforts should be made to add to their efficiency, lessen their detectability, and increase their number. Acts of simple sabotage, multiplied by tens of thousands of friend-saboteurs, can be an effective weapon against governments and corporations, and therefore against the international State itself. Slashing tires, draining fuel tanks, spreading rumors, starting arguments, encouraging bad decisions in the workplace, short-circuiting electric systems, and abrading machine parts will waste materials, manpower, and resources. Occurring on a wide scale, simple sabotage will be a constant and tangible drag on the efforts of the State to appear omnipotent and omnipresent. It is arguable that the prime mission of the friend-saboteur is to facilitate the failure of the State's governmental systems by using the systems themselves, and then, when the time is right, to set the stage for selective irregular warfare to strike individual elements of the State.

Simple sabotage may also have a quick return of investment on secondary results of more or less value. The widespread practice of simple sabotage will harass and demoralize administrators, bureaucrats, and their police enforcers, and may disrupt their lives to the point that they make even more foolish choices than they would have otherwise. Further, success may embolden the friend-saboteur eventually to find colleagues who can assist him in sabotage of greater dimensions from inside the departments he is targeting. Finally, the very practice of simple sabotage by friends embedded in government and key corporations may encourage these individuals to identify themselves actively with an alliance of friends, the Lego Distribution Network, or other groups, and establish a local committee of friends to further our efforts in the deconstruction of the State and its puppet governments and crony corporations.

(1-4) When?

If our grandfathers were half the men we imagine them to have been, they would have already completed this task. And if their grandfathers before them had been half the men they imagined them to be, our grandfathers would not have had the opportunity to pass this burden to us. Now we stand, thousands of years bound in slavery to the State, with the choice of passing this Hideous Beast on for our grandchildren to serve, or being the men we ought to be by once and for all times, freeing humanity. Once you have become aware of the Beast, this is the choice; to voluntarily join in resisting or to voluntarily remain bound. Therefore only the individual can decide when he has had enough of being a slave and when he is morally obligated to set himself free.

(1-5) How?

History has shown that working within the confines of the laws that governments have manufactured has never and can never do anything but perpetuate the immoral system that protects and nurtures the State. History has further shown that to confront governments using traditional revolutionary tactics only serves to replace one tyrannical government with another, and again this strengthens the international State.

Historically, the third option people have attempted repeatedly over millennia is to attempt to escape the State by moving to a location where the tentacles of governments have yet to reach. The State has defeated this tactic by continually growing and systematically engulfing and devouring those free people, often through open slaughter of whole populations. Finally the desperate have, on many occasions, attempted to fortify some kind of stronghold and wait for a messianic or apocalyptic deliverance from the heavens. Of course this has never worked and usually ends in a regrettable blood bath, leaving only a hand full of survivors at best.

It is with hard examples from history that this three-pronged method, aboveground activists, underground simple sabotage, and ethics-based selective irregular warfare, has developed. Using lessons learned and finding the best practices from all available sources, this manual seeks to encourage both actions and observations that will stimulate the improvement of our efforts. We know that the education of the masses in understanding freedom is paramount, and the freedom we offer must be sold to humanity in the marketplace of ideas. But we also understand that so long as the coercive State appears to fulfill its promises of economic growth, security, prosperity, infrastructure, and justice, while appearing omnipotent, omnipresent, and omniscient, we have a distinct sales disadvantage. It is only through the failure of the State that the market will seek an alternative. Therefore we seek to be the mechanism that drives the failure of the State. We do this understanding that our enemy will not hesitate to murder on a grand and hideous scale to maintain its position. Therefore, limited by our commitment of not initiating aggression upon peaceful people nor upon the property of said people, we must endeavor to find ways to become the catalyst that begins the lethal reaction that will dissolve the foundations of the State. We must be the ones who take the shoes from our feet and cram them into the gears of oppression, bringing this machine to a halt.

(1-6) Who?

A small varmint that can spoil one vine undetected
Can ruin the vineyard

Who has government enslaved? Who is the child, the brother, the mother, the friend, of someone government has murdered or unjustly imprisoned? Who has tried to start a business, but was overwhelmed by regulations or taxes? Who has tried to catch a fish to feed his children, but didn't have the proper government permission slip? Who has struggled through the death of a parent only to find government has ravished the estate and left the family in debt? Who has ever looked in the rearview mirror of their automobile and has been gripped by fear knowing the cop behind them can rape them and beat them to death and never be punished for his crime? Who has had their life turned upside down by an uncaring, half-wit, dead-eyed government bureaucrat just doing his job? Who has never been directly confronted by authorities, yet has compassion for the downtrodden and empathy for the victims of oppression? These are potentially our friends, supporters, and possibly even our fellow saboteurs. And with every filmed police brutality, with every repressive act of government, with every asset seizure, with every drone that kills a child, the State creates more of them every single day.

Who takes orders at the restaurant? Who fills prescriptions at the pharmacy? Who empties the trash at the office? Who stands guard at the factory, late into the night? Who installs the wires in the new government courthouse? Who repairs the heating/cooling system at the police station? Who routes the airplanes over the vast expanses of the prairies? Who programs the traffic lights that keep the surges of life flowing through the city during rush hours? Who drives the ambulance that brings the suffering to the hospital? Who bravely walks into the burning building to save a life? Who is the trusted IT specialist that has access to the network that holds the video that the world needs to see? The answer is the same as above. The answer is; it is us. The abused. The victims of government and those sympathetic and the empathetic to our plight. And the State creates more of us every single day.

We are everywhere. We have no Great Leader and we must never have a Great Leader. We are regular people living regular lives.

We write programs that allow desk-top computer-controlled milling machines to cut untraceable parts for military grade weapons in the tool shed of the farmer in Kansas. We write the virus that invades the government computer network to create back doors. We mow the lawn at the Senator's home while his children nap in their nursery. We hold the oxygen mask snuggly against the face of the city mayor as he drifts into a state that allows him to comfortably have that important surgery. We push the cart and deliver the interoffice mail to the desks of the intelligence analysts who study the results of drone strikes. We inspect the breaks of the fleet vehicles in the motor pool that serves the lobbyist that will meet with the Ways and Means Committee this afternoon. We do these things. We allow the whole system around us to continue and we can stop that entire system or critical aspects of it, any time we decide it needs to stop. This is who we are and this is what we can do. And the State creates more of us every single day.

2. FRIENDS, ENEMIES, NEUTRALS, AND TRUST

If you know your enemy and know yourself, you can win many battles without loss
If you only know yourself, but not your enemy, you may win or you may lose
If you know neither yourself nor your enemy, you will always pay the price

It is imperative that we have solid definitions when it comes to who we can and who we cannot trust. Networks of saboteurs must be secure in order to succeed, and they can only be as secure as the local individual saboteur is secure. That can only be achieved through careful and thorough vetting of our network of friends and supporters. In aboveground activism, suspicions and paranoia can be divisive and can harm a movement. But in an underground movement focusing on activities that can land the individual in a government cage or worse, there is no such thing as being too careful. We can allow no deviation of principles, no questionable characters, and whenever possible, no means of compromising the individual in their private lives. That is not to say that every friend-saboteur be a perfect angelic being. It does mean that every reasonable effort must be made to insure that the underground network is safe from infiltrators, the incompetent, the desperate, the loud mouth, the big shot, and short thinking emotional reactionaries.

As the old saying goes; a chain is only as strong as its weakest link. And the shorter that chain the less likely it is to have a weak link. Local friend-saboteurs are safest when they work alone. Working with one more saboteur doubles the likelihood of detection, and adding a third friend to the group triples the chances. It can be argued that many hands make the task light, but when it comes to trust, the smaller the circle the better.

Saboteur networks should be distributed networks with each friend-saboteur connected to several others, without any being dependent on a central organization. The network should not depend on one universal method of communication. For example, some can connect through secure internet chat, while others can talk at physical meeting places and physical drop points, and others can connect through secure network-only telephones (not carrier based telephone systems, but dedicated secure networks using dedicated network-only portable phones). In any event, meetings of medium to large groups should be discouraged, and any form of open communication should be through selective non-specific wording and code words. For example, rather than referring to a friend-saboteur by name, describe him by some other means, such as; "Our friend with the little brown dog." And rather than saying; "I have hacked into the police chief's computer." one could say; "That one fat pig left his back door open so I took a looked around." As silly and cartoonish as these examples may sound, they are time tested methods, and the more a crew of activists uses them the better they will get at being very specific while staying incredibly vague. In other words, this method works!

(2-1) Friends

The fool chases every colorful butterfly
The wise man paints himself in the dull colors of the forest
And quietly waits for the stag that will feed his family

Trusted friends of freedom must be enemies of slavery, enemies of aggression, and enemies of all who would steal from us, cage us, and kill us.

The friend of freedom can make no excuse for collectivism and government domination. The friend of freedom is not a nationalist, a racist, a bigot, nor any other form of collectivist who would seek to judge his fellow man based on anything other than the man himself. The friend of freedom is a true abolitionist and a voluntaryist. He doesn't pick and choose what "rights" the government should "grant" or "protect". The friend of freedom knows that government can only suppress rights, and it can give nothing to anyone unless it stole it from someone else first. The friend of freedom should express to the world his unique brand of liberty primarily though his own deeds and secondarily through his words. The friend of freedom's life, in-and-of-itself should be an act of witness, and "evangelism" should be an afterthought if it is to be engaged in at all. After all, freedom is the natural condition of humanity. It is our default setting. Freedom needs no outlandish televangelists. In actuality freedom is the enemy of the religion of Statism, but it is not a competing religion and it needs no phony hucksters selling it for the price of a donation.

The vast majority of friends of freedom will be content to seek their own freedom in their own life through avoiding government agents or attempting to get-along as best they can with the system we currently have. They don't like the system, but many feel there is little if anything they can do about it. They have families and busy lives and their primary goal is to survive, and we wish them well. Some will be driven to speak-out in some way or express their frustration with the current system through writing or public speaking or though some other peaceful activism. We need these activists and we honestly do wish them well. However there will be some of these friends who will not be content to avoid conflict. There will be some who will possess a fire burning inside them, and that fire will seek a different path. From this last group we must carefully select our friend-saboteurs and teach them of our mission. From this radical group the Legos will be spread across the carpet in anticipation of that moment. Then in the middle of the night the State will encounter that immovable object, and the State will be revealed, not as an omnipotent god, but as fragile and weak, crumbling to its knees for all to see.

This we will do.

(2-1.1) There are friends, and then there are friends.

Friend-saboteurs are a very special type of anarchists. For most peaceful anarchists, the thought of actively and intentionally damaging property or personally targeting individuals is not what they have come to know as acceptable behavior. The vast majority of them will object to our type of activism. Some will be so offended that they may present a threat of exposure to the friend-saboteur. Because of this gap in understanding, it should not be the role of the saboteur to recruit for the cause of simple-sabotage. Rather we should let nature take its course and allow friend-saboteurs to develop at their own speed, as weeds in the garden of the State. Then, when we are relatively sure of their intentions, it is best if a non-saboteur friend approaches them with something like this manual or other material introducing the concept.

There is a role for every like-minded person as a friend-saboteur, however ideally the perfect friend-saboteur will not be burdened by family members that the government can arrest and use as leverage against him. He will not be the outspoken radical known for his objections to the State. He will not be the confrontational anarchist with an arrest record for activism, "420" slogans on his shirt, neon blue dreadlocks, and a 000 gauge nose piercing. He will not have a bumper sticker on his car that reads; "Bad Pig! No Donut!" or "End Welfare Abuse, Shoot A Pig!" In short, the ideal friend-saboteur will look like the teller at your bank, the head nurse on the cardiac floor, or the friendly local package delivery driver in the brown truck. Each of these stealth anarchists are worth more than an army of angry adult-children dressed in black, setting trash cans on fire and throwing rocks at cops. Each dedicated stealth anarchist/friend-saboteur is worth a hundred legions of video warriors asking strangers on the street about the value of silver so they can laugh at the uneducated while pumping up their view count on social media.

In short, the ideal friend-saboteur should be invisible to the State, ingenious in action, wise in discretion, and long on patience. But few of us are perfect. Sometimes wisdom and patience can win the day all by themselves.

(2-2) Enemies

The enemy of my enemy
My well be a far more dangerous enemy

(2-2.1) The Great Enemy of Humanity

*To be ignorant of what happened before you were born
Is to remain forever a child*

To understand the State you could think in terms of theology and mythology. The State would appear to be the unholy trinity of government, select corporations, and central banking, served by their demonic lackeys the media/entertainment/circuses, select clergy and select intelligentsia. In fact these are the idols, the temples, the priests, and the tools of the State, not the State itself. The State, whether real or imagined, is the deity in the minds of humans that inspires those humans to behave in a way that supports and perpetuates the above stated trinity and its ghoulish angels. The State would be easily killed if it were simply a government or a bank. But it is not that. It dwells in the minds of countless actors worldwide, and it constantly shifts, morphs, and mutates in order to maintain its existence and dominance. Today corporations control governments and banks control corporations, but this relationship is fluid. Tomorrow the clergy may be back on top or governments could regain preeminence. The pecking order doesn't matter, only the Beast matters and it dwells in the hearts of men, not in the institutions.

Another way of viewing our enemy, the State, is by considering the study of Memetics under a Dawkinsian interpretation. In this view the State is an inorganic being, a unit of culture rather than a unit of carbon, that lives in the human mind and leaps from human to human as a form of reproduction. Like a virus, memes can range from harmless or a mild irritant, to a deadly infection without cure. Also much like a virus, some humans appear to be immune or resistant to particular memes while some have no resistance at all. In the case of the State, if you consider the incredible body count amassed during its current incarnation, roughly from 1600 CE (the birth of corporations and modern banking) to present, it would rank as the most deadly virus ever know to infect humans. However unlike a virus, a meme (in this case, the State) can cause an infected human or humans to kill non-infected humans in massive numbers. Some estimates exceed 250,000,000 deaths just by governments during the 20th century alone, and that staggering number doesn't include war. Read that again, 250 million people murdered by governments in 100 years and that doesn't include war! This is our enemy!

Whether a deity or a meme, the State exists in the mind of the infected believer and has now grown capable of exterminating the entire human race, along with a good portion, if not all, life on this planet. The State is even the enemy of those most dedicated to it, they are simply too blinded or too greedy to see this truth. In some people the infection is so complete that they will willingly sacrifice themselves, their children, and everything they own and love for their Precious, the State. Therefore this is not an enemy to take lightly or to attack foolishly.

Once we determine that our primary enemy is not a single person, it is not an institution, it is not a political party, and it is not "capitalism" or "socialism", but it is a belief system that inspires millions of followers worldwide, then and only then can we develop a successful plan to defeat it. That plan must first and foremost take into account our own strengths and our weaknesses, and determine the strengths and weaknesses of our enemy. Each of us must then decide our own role and weigh the individual price to engage this enemy. Only the fool begins to build a house without determining the cost and assessing himself to assure he can afford the construction. Only after accomplishing these steps, we may engage our enemy on the field of battle that we choose with the weapons, timing, and rules that we choose. We expose our self to the enemy only in the way that we choose to expose our self. And then when the fray is upon us we must fight without mercy, without emotion, and with no thought of ever giving quarter or settling for any form of peace that doesn't include the complete death of our enemy, the State. Anything less and this Beast will simply regroup, shape-shift, and return upon us stronger than it has ever been. This is the nature of our enemy, the State.

(2-2.1.1) The Strength of the State

The story of the State can be understood by examining the story of the Lernaean Hydra of ancient mythology. The Hydra cannot be killed by a single decapitation, as it just grows more heads from the bloody stump of the last head. Its blood is so caustic that one drop will dissolve the best armor and its breath will kill a strong man.

Indications are that this, like the stories of the ancient Titans, was originally a folk tale warning of the dangers of governments. The interesting aspect of this story is that the founders of the Greek states perverted this story to justify their bloody government regimes. In the myth, the gods brought forth the only person who could defeat the Hydra, that being the great hero Hercules. Yes, Hercules was the savior of humanity. The same bloody Hercules that murdered his own family. As luck would have it, most of the ancient kings of the Greek cities just happened to be direct descendants of this Great Man, thus justifying the reign of each king, or so they told their subjects. This is how the State operates. When people come to realize what a hideous monster the government is, the State provides a Great Man as the Deliverer. The Great Man destroys the monster and sets up a new government. That's why we need strong government headed by a Great Man, otherwise there would be a strong government headed by a monstrous beast. And yet, that Great Man is always the puppet of the true Beast, the State.

The State exists in the minds of hundreds of millions of faithful believers worldwide. Estimates are that there are currently some 350,000 humans born every day. That means the State can sacrifice vast numbers of believers and "neutrals" (see description below) without seriously weakening its base of existence. Additionally, a common belief among faithful State supporters is the idea that the earth is over-populated. Whether true or not, the existence of State followers who not only believe this but are also in positions of influence and authority means that there are people with decision making power who would be willing to exterminate unimaginable quantities of their fellow humans in order to keep the State alive and functioning. And their fanatical belief system demands such sacrifices, as has been clearly demonstrated throughout their history. When a sane free-minded person considers the State under these terms, it's difficult to grasp the extent that those in power will go in order to maintain their power structure. However when we think about the strengths of the State, this is the exact thing we must take into consideration. The State has no love of humanity. It feels no empathy. It is incapable of knowing fear. It thinks of humans no more than a virus thinks about its current host. Without blinking and on command, the faithful followers will throw the switches, lock the targets, and turn the keys that will incinerate cities full of people, sending poisonous waves of radioactive dust into the atmosphere to continue killing for decades. This is our enemy, the State.

Such an enemy cannot be reasoned with, cannot be threatened, cannot be intimidated, cannot be bluffed, cannot be bribed, cannot be negotiated with, and will never stop until he dominates every single human or kills them all in the process. Such an enemy is willing to send any quantity of young foolish followers into battle to either die or murder waves and waves of both combatants and non-combatants alike. Such an enemy will round up millions for extermination on the hope of killing a hand full in the resistance. This enemy sees with hundreds of millions of eyes, and any idea we can come up with has already passed through a hundred million of its brains. This is our enemy, this is the State.

These are just some of the strengths of the State, but this list can continue. He has almost unlimited wealth. A stronghold cannot be built that he cannot destroy. Hiding from him is near impossible. He can touch almost every electronic communication. He has information about almost every human. He constantly seeks more details about everyone. And he will not stop so long as he has believers who love power.

This is our enemy, the State.

(2-2.1.2) The Weak Points of the State

A child can crush the spider with his hand
Yet no king can possess a throne room that she cannot invade
An emperor can command a million slaves
Yet when he sleeps she may walk across his brow
A president may order the destruction of cities
But he is not immune to her venom
In the dark corner, when the moment is right, her egg sacks open
And thousands of her children invade the palace
And there are more of us every day

The Federal Reserve in the United States and its IMF cohorts around the world provide the lion's share of the funding that our enemy the State uses to continue its dominance of humanity. The blockchain and her children, cryptocurrencies, are like millions of spiders spinning webs and moving about as they see fit, doing what they want where they want, in spite of every effort to stop them. Some find the blockchain terrifying, some find her complicated, and some fail to notice her at all. She is a beautiful marvel if you see her with the right eyes. However, on her own she is not enough to kill the Beast. We must look further.

Physical components of the State; governments, central banks, crony corporations, the military industrial complex, the main stream media, and the main stream entertainment industry, all possess the same weakness in their structure. They are all based on collectivism, central planning, and constant internal power struggles, to maintain order. The phrase "dog-eat-dog" was coined to describe their inner workings. The image of the snake swallowing its tail epitomizes the turmoil that is indicative of the components of the State. They are a serpent constantly devouring itself. A fake perpetual motion machine that always consumes its internal parts to maintain the illusion of functionality. On the physical/economic level, the only thing that keeps this Beast alive is the continuous stream of flesh, blood, and sweat, harvested from the productive of the world, and fed into the flames of its belly. And that internal turmoil is the weak point in the armor of the State where we must drive our lance. When you understand this weak point you will see that it exists in every aspect of the physical components of the State.

(2-2.1.2.01) Using the corporation as an example.

Many large corporations are incredibly delicate. Assuming the corporation is doing well, making money, and stable in its sector, there is a good likelihood it depends on government contracts, a government provided quasi-monopoly, corporate welfare, or some other kind of government provided advantage.

In other words, the corporation depends on the political model of taxation/theft and cronyism to survive. No matter its appearance of stability, if you look closely you will see that the actual workforce has little-to-no motivation to work hard, strive to improve, seek innovation, nor function efficiently. The "best" workers are the few who show up to work every day, don't talk back to managers, and don't steal. The go-getter, the over-producer is seen as a threat to his fellow worker and sometimes even a threat to his slackard-boss. The corporate boss, on every level, has a built-in motivation to keep the productive workers down the ladder in production positions while advancing the less productive up the corporate ladder. This is a well-documented phenomenon called The Peter Principle. Consider the following example:

Supervisor Bob has 10 workers. He is one of 5 peer-level supervisors, each of which has 10 workers. So: 50 workers, 5 supervisors.

Bob and his 4 supervisor peers answer to a manager named Tom and Tom is one of 5 managers.

Tom informs Bob and his peers that a manager spot has opened, and one of Bob's peers, Joe has been chosen to move up. Bob is being considered as next-in-line to move up to manager. Tom tells Bob that Bob may choose one of the 50 workers to be the new supervisor, replacing Joe.

Does Bob select the top worker, knowing this new supervisor will compete with Bob for the next manager spot? Or does Bob pick one of the workers who is barely competent so that the new supervisor will not out-perform Bob and not be chosen to pass Bob, becoming the new manager?

Of course the answer is that Bob will likely choose someone who will not be a threat to Bob's advancement. Bob will not choose the best worker. Bob may even select the worst worker to replace Joe. *Interruption!* At this point in the example the question becomes; why did Tom choose Joe to move up to manager? Did Tom pick the best supervisor or did Tom pick the one he knew was barely competent so that Tom wouldn't be threatened in his next advancement?

This is critical in understanding corporate structure. If you are confused or didn't follow this demonstration, please read it again or look up The Peter Principle and acquaint yourself with this phenomenon, because it is important to knowing our enemy!

Now multiply this formula over every level of the corporate structure from the janitorial staff to the board of directors. Add into the equation internal politics, jealousy, personal animosity, nepotism, and personal relationships. The final result is a business model that can only compete with other inept crony corporations. In an actual free market, unencumbered by government favoritism and advantages, such a business would quickly crumble.

Once again, the above described business structure is the pattern that the physical components of the State are all designed to function under. So the underpinnings of the State, the feet of the idol as it were, are made of clay. Simple "slacktivism" in and of itself can be a tremendous threat to the stability of the Beast. The great redemption in this revelation is that the truth of the above described weakness of the State is already well known to vast numbers of State supporters. All we need to do is shine the light of mass-system failure onto this flaw, while providing a logical solution.

(2-2.1.2.02) The Corporation Stifles Innovation and Progress

The following story is one example of the incompetence of the State and the vulnerability that it displays. However this is just one example. With a little thought and effort these flaws can be revealed in every product and service that the State, through its governments and crony-corporatism, monopolistically force upon us.

In the 1960s and 1970s many respected construction engineers began speaking out against the use of overhead electrical transmission lines as opposed to underground lines. Although the topic remains debatable today, the advantages of underground lines are significant. They are demonstrably more reliable and safer, yet the utility companies were resistant to widely adopting the new method. Their primary reasons; their existing infrastructure was committed to the overhead model, and installation of underground lines cost 5-15 times more than overhead. Those arguing in favor of underground pointed out that construction companies could be charged the price difference and simply pass the cost to the consumers through higher construction prices. These would be disproportionately covered by business rather than individual home owners.

However the utility industry resisted and lobbied to stop local, state, and federal regulations requiring underground lines. In the background, and less obvious to the casual observer, was the fact that the powerful timber and coal interests were raking in a fortune selling creosote injected wooden poles to the utility giants, and they were also lobbing against the underground utilities at the same time. Because of antiquated subsidies and regulations regarding the expansion of the electrical grid dating back to the 1930s, the utility companies had a tax sponsored incentive to resist the underground method in favor of the overhead. So as the utility giants expanded their electrical grid through the 1980s and 1990s, they stayed with the technology of the 1880s funded by laws of the 1930s, rather than adapting and modernizing to the current state of the industry.

Remember the preceding paragraph the next time an ice storm or a hurricane leaves half a million Americans without power for a couple weeks. Now think about what would happen if a small dedicated group of fanatics decided to drive around the countryside with a rifle taking out remote transformers. Such a situation would be uncomfortable in the southwest during the summer, but could be considered mass murder if it happened around the Great Lakes in February. And yet, isn't that what the State has done by incentivizing the overhead lines throughout regions that regularly suffer crushing ice storms?

Some may ask; "If the market is so great why can't it provide a better solution than 1880s style overhead wires or expensive trenching and underground lines?"

Late 1990s fuel cell technology using existing natural gas infrastructure, demonstrated private ownership of generators could provide cheap, clean, quiet, reliable, electricity to new home construction in North America, adding roughly $10,000 to the sale price of each new home, but recovering that amount in utility cost savings, while virtually eliminating power outages. At the time several small start-up companies were competing to get these generators on the market.

Please note here; these were not magic free energy machines, fuel cells are established reliable electric generators.

Once sales of the fuel cells caught on in the construction market, projections indicated the cost of a home fuel cell generator may have fallen by 50% by 2002, making them widely available and affordable as a retrofit in the booming home-renovation sector. Big energy companies saw the profit potential and began absorbing the small start-up companies, but the potential for the consumer still seemed limitless. However, energy giants Enron, GE, Berkshire Hathaway, Boone Pickens Capital Management, and others clashed in 2000/2001 resulting in the fall of Enron, the evaporation of incredible amounts of false capital, and the hope of energy independent housing practically vanished, while continued mass-dependency on the 1880s style power grid was almost guaranteed for another generation due to the same factors involved in resisting the innovation of underground utilities two decades earlier. This example of corporate mishandling of technology could easily be seen as evidence of some grand conspiracy to control the energy market. However no conspiracy is needed to explain this tragedy. This is simply the way giant corporations and the existing capital management systems work. In theory, government regulators should prevent events like this from happening, however the opposite is true. The history of modern banking/corporate regulatory practices shows conclusively that this is exactly how the system is designed to function.

This example provides an insight into two distinct and separate weaknesses of the State. The first weakness can be exploited through education and propaganda. Unfortunately the Enron scandal is complicated and as you attempt to explain it to the average State believer his eyes will likely glaze over in boredom and disinterest long before your point can be made. If you're knowledgeable of the intricate details of this massive scandal, and if you have the skill set to tell this tail without your listeners dropping into a comatose state, you may be able to convince your listener that the whole corporate/government system is designed to inhibit innovation while draining the maximum amount of wealth from the productive sector and funneling that wealth into the banking/investment sector. Good luck with that, since the Enron scandal has been told over and over with almost no one even mentioning the fuel cell aspect of the story.

It may be easier to expose the flaw in being dependent upon the banking/corporation/government structure that provides the energy to your home that keeps your children alive during the winter. The promise from the State is that the State provides for us what the market by itself cannot. Not only is that a lie, the State actually provides a very unstable supply of overpriced energy. The energy grid is incredibly delicate due to the fact that it is the product of 135 years of central planning. It is rife with flaws, weak design, over-burdened bottle-necks, and inefficiency. The power companies are riddled with corruption and stagnant thinking, and shackled by regulations that stopped making any sense 75 years ago if they ever made sense at all. So we have this propaganda/education opportunity, but only if it is explained correctly or demonstrated in practical terms. But who will listen and why will they listen so long as the lights work?

Thus we have the second weakness provided by this example. The State's power grid, while keeping the people of North America alive every winter, is incredibly delicate and yet it is a source of faith in the existing system. Consider this: The Nile River was the source of life for old Egypt. If the Nile rises every time Pharaoh sacrifices to the gods, then every time the Nile rises it proves the divinity of Pharaoh. However if Pharaoh makes the sacrifice but the Nile fails, faith in Pharaoh weakens. If Pharaoh promises to solve the Nile problem but the Nile fails again, even after painful sacrifice by the people, more will question their faith in Pharaoh. Pharaoh's reaction will almost certainly be to double-down on the sacrifice, at the cost of the people. The lesson here is that so long as the evidence seems to support the State's narrative, the believers have no reason to question their faith. But when the system fails and fails again in spite of the State's efforts and promises, faith can be shaken. This is the single largest flaw in the armor of the State; it can't provide what it promises. We have electricity during the winter in spite of the State, not because of it.

Again, the examples stated here are indicative of every product and service the State claims monopolistic right to supply. In every case, the State is vulnerable to a three pronged attack, if that attack is done correctly. Prong one involves the careful infiltration of the manpower of the target.

In other words, anarchists employed at the points of weakness. Friend-saboteurs should develop a functional understanding of the infrastructure of the target. Controlled probing and testing provide information on target reactions and responses. Weaknesses are discovered and prioritized. Simple acts of sabotage harass the target while setting up a larger attack. During this time the second prong of the attack begins to come into play; that being education and propaganda. Aboveground activists preach against the centrally planned State behemoth, warning that such structures are unstable and that society should not rely on something as undependable as the State. As the aboveground activists loudly predict disaster, the underground saboteurs provide the disaster. When the Nile fails and fails again, and Pharaoh reacts with violence, increased confiscations, and oppression, thus faith in the State weakens. And Then!

Eventually the people begin to understand that there is no connection between the Nile and the State. The pharaoh and all his ministers are nothing but a violent gang of thieves. People stop making excuses for them and they stop protecting them. At this point the third prong strikes with precision and removes the human leadership of the State, thus ends the war.

It should be noted that the timing of the third prong is critical. If you strike too soon or are too obvious, you garner sympathy for the State actors. If you strike too late you may miss the critical moment of vulnerability and you may have to repeat the first two operations. It should also be noted that there can be no public connection between the friend-saboteurs and the aboveground activists. The aboveground activists must consistently denounce sabotage or dismiss accusations of sabotage as crazy conspiracy theories concocted by desperate State actors to hide their incompetence. Do not miss this important point; when State actors blame anarchists for well executed sabotage, aboveground activists can claim the statists are crazy conspiracy theorists. Finally; the third prong in this example should be recognized as the selective irregular warfare mentioned earlier. There should never be a public connection between selective irregular warfare and the aboveground activists nor the network of friend-saboteurs. These must appear to be separate unrelated entities. In best practice, there should never be an acknowledgment of the existence of the friend-saboteurs nor of the existence of the irregular warriors. Largely, their success depends on their invisibility.

When done in one sector of industry or one sector of the economy, or one geographical location, the above procedure can be damaging to the State. When coordinated to strike many sectors at once the truth of the State will be revealed for all to see. If done correctly, coordinated on a world-wide scale, this procedure will only need to be done once.

The State is like a great Colossus on a pedestal, made of steel and crowned in gold, but standing on feet of clay. It's not the job of the friend-saboteur to melt the steel. After all, Molotov cocktails won't melt steel beams! It is only our job to make fissures in the clay. Gravity will do the rest.

(2-2.2) Our Human Enemies

Fighting the government doesn't make you an anarchist.
Some who fight authority do so only because they wish to have the power of the authority for themselves.

There are as many flavors of enemies as there are enemies. It's important not to fall into collectivist thinking, either in the positive nor the negative direction. In other words, one should reject the idea of assuming everyone who fights a current government is a friend, just like one should reject the idea that everyone who is not a philosophically perfect anarchist is an enemy. Many people can do things that would seem to place them in the category of friend but if they were to obtain the slightest political power they would quickly become a more dangerous enemy than the ones currently in charge. Likewise a person can take actions that would seem to flag them as enemies, but they are simply confused neutrals making bad choices. So before we label someone as an enemy we have to be sure of their intentions. Also in labeling an enemy, the input of multiple opinions is valuable. In short, be slow to judge, as this judgment can have deadly consequences. As important as it is to discriminate when we choose who to trust, we must discriminate when choosing who to condemn.

Having said that, we must also reject some commonly held beliefs. It is often said; keep your friends close and your enemies closer. This old saying comes to us in modern times from the writings of Niccolò di Bernardo dei Machiavelli, an Italian politician, diplomat, and philosopher. Basically an advisor to our enemy. Not to say we can't learn from Machiavelli, we most definitely can. But Machiavelli was not writing from the perspective of ripping the prince down, he was writing from the perspective of keeping the prince in power. Machiavelli was advising a prince on how to behave in a way to maintain his monopoly of violence. That is the opposite of our design. Good advice for a prince is not by default good advice for everyone. We must be more like the spider mentioned in section 2-2.1.2 above. Ideally we want to be near the prince, if possible serving him a bowl of soup or driving him to his dentist appointment, but we should try to be in that position in a way that he doesn't notice we exist or doesn't recognize us as the threat that we are.

As a general rule, the use of physical violence upon the person or persons of our enemies should be avoided by the friend-saboteur. This is not a hard rule set in stone, it is guidance that should be taken into consideration when making that decision. This should not be taken to mean there should never be violence used against our enemies, it is simply stating that wisdom should dictate when to strike and what method will provide the best result. Eventually there will be physical violence upon specific targets by those engaging in irregular warfare, but we won't be covering that in this section of this manual. For more on irregular warfare see the publication: Sedition Subversion and Sabotage Field Manual No. 1, Ethics Based Irregular Warfare.

For our purposes in this section of this manual, we can classify the three types of enemies that the friend-saboteur should concern himself with:

1) Those who issue orders to rob, intimidate, cage, maim, and kill to maintain the State's murderous grip on humanity. These people should be our primary human targets when using simple sabotage. They may be high level bureaucrats, politicians, military officers, judges, or high level law enforcement. If it's possible to positively identify the "shadow government actors" then they would be at the top of this category. Once again, as tempting as it is to resort to direct violence, wisdom must rule our actions. Our main goal is to disrupt their plans, distract

their attention, and generally place Legos in the carpet of their life to keep them stumbling in the dark.

2) Those who choose to obey and execute above stated orders: These people are the front line police, military, prison guards, mid-to-low level bureaucrats, building inspectors, health inspectors, children's services agents, federal letter-agency thugs, and every government actor that directly interfaces with the public to enforce the arbitrary will of governments. These are individually our most dangerous enemies. They are the ones most likely to directly use violence upon the innocent.

3) Those who knowingly facilitate the order givers and the order executers: This is the widest group with the widest definition, therefor the most difficult to classify accurately. It includes main stream media writers, personalities, and news directors. It's the corporate leaders that oversee the military industrial complex, the central banking complex, and secondary workers in the prison industrial complex. It's the mid-level government bureaucrats, the mid-level corporate deal makers, the clergy that have sold their soul to the all mighty State. It is the software writers, hardware developers, and hackers that betray the entire information technology sector while doing the dirty work for their State masters by facilitating the surveillance industry. In short, these people are the willful hands and fingers of the State

(2-3) Neutrals

The word "neutral" has its origin in the same word as "neuter". Neuter is the castration of a male pet, and in the context of this discussion, that may be the best possible definition of those who are neither our friends nor our enemies. One of the most successful methods of the State throughout history has been to virtually neuter the bulk of the population, leaving them as little more than docile house pets. The most serious danger neutrals present to us is their tendency to bark and whine, alerting their masters as to our presence or our activities. Sometimes it's easy to confuse these eunuchs with actual enemies, but it's important to understand the distinction. We must never aggress upon the neutrals. We must always keep in mind that they are victims of the State. It is our job to set them free, not punish them for their lack of understanding. Never compromise this foundational principle; rights do not depend on knowledge nor on understanding. Rights cannot be deigned a person based on ignorance.

Therefore we must always treat the neutrals as non-combatants and grant them the same respect as we do our friends. Their lives, their safety, and their property, must be preserved and respected.

Final thoughts on neutrals; as they are many of us have been. As we are now they may someday be. That said, neutrals can never be trusted. Never, so long as they remain neutrals, can they be trusted! Even after they awake, former neutrals should be carefully observed and tested. It's only as they prove themselves with small things that you may begin to trust them on bigger things. However, always use caution. The effects of the State can linger.

3. MOTIVATING THE SABOTEUR

To incite our friend to the active practice of simple sabotage and to keep him practicing that sabotage over sustained periods is a special problem.

Simple sabotage is often an act which our friend performs according to his own initiative and inclination. Acts of destruction do not bring him any personal gain and may be completely foreign to his habitually libertarian attitude toward people, property, and services. Also the tendency to respect property may be a particular burden when encouraging our friend to do that which may seem contrary to the disposition of a good and peaceful person. Objections regarding the destruction of property, while seemingly noble, are based on a wrongheaded understanding of the violent nature of the State and the stolen hoards and possessions the State has amassed. Also in reference to slacktivism, purposefully acting stupid is contrary to human nature. He may frequently need guidance, encouragement, stimulation, assurance, information, and suggestions regarding feasible methods of using that kind of simple sabotage.

(3-1) Personal Motives

(3-1.1)

The ordinary person very probably has no immediate personal motive for committing simple sabotage. Instead, he must be made to anticipate indirect personal gain, such as might come with the fall of the State or destruction of the ruling elite and their minions.

Gains should be stated as specifically as possible for the area addressed: simple sabotage will hasten the day when Commissioner X and his deputies Y and Z will be thrown out, when particularly obnoxious regulations and prohibitions will be abolished, when taxation will end, and so on. Abstract verbalizations about personal liberty, freedom of the press, and so forth, will not be convincing in most parts of the world. In many areas they will not even be comprehensible.

(3-1.2)

Since the effect of his own acts of sabotage are limited, the saboteur may become discouraged unless he feels that he is a member of a larger, though unseen, group of like-minded saboteurs operating against the Enemy of Humanity throughout the world. Several methods can be used to encourage the friend-saboteur. Helping them gain access to the dark web or guiding them toward podcasts or other sources of information may help. Along these lines, statements praising the effectiveness of simple sabotage can be collected and then published on the dark web, on freedom radio, on podcasts, and other forms of subversive media. Estimates of the proportion of the population engaged in sabotage can be disseminated. Instances of successful sabotage already are talked about negatively by the mouth of the State, so using their news reports while giving them a positive spin can be of great encouragement and should not be that difficult. However all care should be taken to avoid exposing the identity and the personal details of our friends. This should always be of the utmost concern. All information disseminated should be continued and expanded while remaining compatible with security and individual safety. Those who understand "OPSEC" should put special effort into helping the friend-saboteur network become as educated as possible on the topic. Once the individual saboteur becomes more knowledgeable on the topic he will be more confident to download material from the internet and utilize the dark net.

(3-1.3)

The next step in motivating the local friend-saboteur is to create a situation in which the friend-saboteur acquires a sense of responsibility and begins to educate others in what he has learned about the art of simple sabotage. Ideally establishing a base of operation where training and encouragement of new friends would develop and branch out with yet more bases of operation. Few things encourage a person to learn their craft as intensely as teaching, since you must learn the craft in order to effectively teach. And as you teach you gain a sense of ownership in your students and in your organization.

(3-2) Encouraging Slacktivism Along With Disruption, and Destruction (D&D)

It should be pointed out to the saboteur where the circumstances are suitable, that he is acting in self-defense against our common enemy, or retaliating against our enemy for other acts of D&D, but in all cases he is a saboteur because he is trying to stop the State from further atrocities upon the innocent, and the faster we destroy the State the more innocent lives we save. Our friend should constantly be reassured that he is not initiating aggression, but is acting in defense of the powerless. Also a reasonable amount of humor in the presentation of suggestions for simple sabotage will relax tensions and fear. Again, and as always, an emphasis of non-aggression against the innocent and respect for true private property must be maintained.

When engaging in slacktivism, the saboteur may have to reverse his thinking, and he should be told this in so many words. Where he formerly thought of keeping his tools sharp, he should now let them grow dull; surfaces that formerly were lubricated now should be sanded; normally diligent, he should now be lazy and careless; and so on. Once he is encouraged to think backwards he'll see many opportunities in his immediate environment which cannot possibly be seen from a distance. A state of mind should be encouraged that anything can be sabotaged, and every little act is a strike against the enemy of humanity.

Among the potential friend-saboteurs who are to engage in D&D, two extreme types may be distinguished. On the one hand, there is the friend who is not technically trained and employed. Wait-staff, trash collectors, janitors, roofers, grounds keepers, meter readers, dog walkers, and anyone in the service industry.

This activist can use specific suggestions as to how he can and should employ D&D as well as details regarding the tools and means by which D&D is safely accomplished. Direct two way communications with someone who has experience in the same field will be tremendously helpful and encouraging. These friend-saboteurs are extremely important in the overall operation since they can be both numerous and, because of their jobs, they can provide critical information to the wider network as to the movements of targets and the daily lives of enemy personnel. They can be as important in gathering information about our targets as they are in actually committing simple sabotage directly.

At the other extreme is the man who is a technician, a specialist, a journeyman, an engineer, a manager, or a system administrator. Positions such as an equipment operator, automobile mechanic, network administrator, electrician, or fire suppression professional are critical for infiltration and for training other saboteurs. Presumably this activist would be able to devise methods of simple sabotage which would be appropriate to his own facilities. However, this man needs to be stimulated to re-orient his thinking in the direction of D&D. Specific examples, which need not be from his own field, should accomplish this. Keeping always in mind, our enemy is the State, its governments and its crony corporations, not the lives and property of those just trying to live their lives in peace.

Various media may be used to disseminate suggestions and information regarding simple sabotage. Portable drives can be used for "drive-drops" where a thumb-drive or the equivalent, can be stashed in a public place. Our friend can sit down at a table, grab the drive from its hidden spot, plug it into his device accessing the info, then put the drive back for the next friend. He may add info to the drive at the same time. Or the drive can simply be picked up and taken to a safe location. A public library, a coffee shop, a highway roadside rest area, or a public park, are all good places for such activity. Other methods may be, as the immediate situation dictates; podcasts using code words and phrases, local freedom radio, blog posts, social media, the dark web, handouts at various gatherings such as concerts, or other methods. Instructions and suggestions may be directed toward specific geographic or occupational areas, or they may be general in scope.

Finally, activists may be trained in the art of simple sabotage in anticipation of a time when they may be able to be directly involved or communicate this information directly to other of our friends, but may not be actively engaged at that time. A sort of sleeper-cell waiting for activation.

(3-3) Safety Measures

The very first thing the friend-saboteur should clearly understand in regards to safety is that, because of the nature of the risks involved and the nature of our struggle, if or when the friend-saboteur is caught by authorities he is on his own. He should understand that although some private attorney or some other benefactor may step forward to help, the most likely scenario will be that his friends and family will renounce him, and no network of activists will be there for support. This should always be on his mind as he considers each and every act of simple sabotage.

The amount of actions carried out by the saboteur will be governed not only by the number of opportunities he sees, but also by the amount of danger he feels. Bad news travels fast, and simple sabotage will be discouraged if friend-saboteurs are being arrested. Also, unlike our enemy the State, we lack an endless supply of young gullible men and women willing to throw away their lives for a cause. Therefore we must see to the safety of those brave friends who are willing to take the tremendous risks involved in direct actions, which are the hallmark of simple sabotage.

It should not be difficult to prepare handouts and other media for the saboteur about the choice of weapons, time, and targets which will help insulate the saboteur against detection and retaliation. Among such suggestions might be the following:

Use materials which appear to be innocent. A pocket knife or a nail file can be carried normally on your person; either is a multi-purpose instrument for creating damage. Matches, pebbles, hair, salt, nails, over-the-counter laxatives, and dozens of other D&D materials can be carried or kept in your living quarters without exciting any suspicion whatever. If you are a worker in a particular trade or industry you can easily carry and keep such things as wrenches, hammers, emery paper, and the like.

Try to commit acts for which large numbers of people could be responsible. For instance, if you blow out the wiring in a factory at a central power box, make sure that almost anyone could have done it. On-the-street sabotage after dark, the type you might be able to carry out against a police car or SUV, is another example of an act for which it would be impossible to blame you if you are careful in your operation. In all cases, careful planning, knowledge of surveillance cameras, advice from the experienced, and secrecy are critical in safely executing any operation of D&D.

Do not be afraid to commit acts for which you might be blamed directly, so long as you do so rarely, and as long as you have a plausible excuse: you dropped your wrench across an electric circuit because of clumsiness. Always be profuse in your apologies. Frequently you can "get away" with such acts under the cover of pretending stupidity, ignorance, over-caution, fear of terrorists or gangs, lack of training, or physical disability.

After you have committed any act of simple sabotage, resist all temptation to wait around and see what happens. Loiterers arouse suspicion. Of course, there are circumstances when it would be suspicious for you to leave. If you commit sabotage on your job, you should naturally stay at your work station so long as it is safe to do so. Also, every friend-saboteur should understand that, as stupid as our enemy appears at times, they do learn and they will adapt to the events we trigger. You may not be able to repeat the same methods and processes of sabotage, so you should always be on the look-out for new methods and unexplored weaknesses in the locations and workplaces to which you have access.

4. TIMING, TARGETS, AND TOOLS

A pack of wolves is quickly seen as a threat
But the little fox comes in the night and takes what he wants

The friend-saboteur cannot be micro-managed. Nor is it reasonable to expect that simple sabotage can be precisely concentrated on specific types of targets according to the requirements of concrete military timelines.

The nature of a distributed operation requires setting the individuals free to act independently as self-starters through self-direction, and trusting that such a structure will produce positive effects. Also attempts to centrally control simple sabotage according to developing local factors could allow our enemy to anticipate the date and area of intensified or slackened subversive activity, by controlling media reports or news announcements that would possibly affect the schemes of those central planners. Doing so could reveal information about a local group which could in turn lead to an infiltration or a trap. However if each individual is encouraged to rely on his own knowledge and experience he will be much more likely to take ownership of his art and develop it more fully. In this way the individual is far more likely to have better instincts in regards to timing and target, than some sabotage boss making decisions from a safe distance. In that sense we can rely on Hayek's "knowledge problem" to work in our favor if no sabotage central planner is directing an operation and we can be equally comforted in knowing that no State central planner can anticipate the actions of our distributed network. That is not to say suggestions across groups should be discouraged. Sabotage suggestions, of course, should be adapted to fit the area where they are to be practiced. Target priorities for general types of situations likewise can be specified, for emphasis at the proper time by the underground press, friends networks, and cooperating propaganda. However, ultimately the individual friend-saboteurs must be self-directed, as they have the best first-hand knowledge of their targets and their environments.

(4-1) Under General Conditions

D&D style simple sabotage is more than malicious mischief, and it should always consist of acts whose results will be detrimental to the materials, communications, secrecy, morale, or manpower of our enemy.

The saboteur should be ingenious in using his every-day equipment. All sorts of tools will present themselves if he looks at his surroundings in a different light.

For example, emery flakes have incredible utility to the saboteur, but at first it may seem unobtainable. However if the saboteur were to pulverize an emery knife sharpener or emery wheel with a hammer, he would find himself with a plentiful supply. Added to a small hobby rock tumbler and set to tumble for a few days and you have a highly effective powder that will destroy almost any moving part that has a bearing surface. Likewise, something like magnesium flakes may seem exotic, yet magnesium fire-starters are readily available at camping supply stores and can be carefully filed to produce the highly flammable flakes. PLEASE NOTE: Do not attempt to use a motorized grinder or a vibratory polisher on a magnesium fire starter unless you want to destroy your work area and set yourself on fire.

Obtaining German dark aluminum powder (a handy additive in fireworks) may seem dangerous to purchase. Even attempting to purchase aluminum powder may be enough to get the wrong kind of attention and a visit from people you really don't want visiting you. Yet German dark aluminum powder can be easily produced with 1 tablespoon fish tank charcoal, a hand full of 1/2-3/4 inch steel ball bearings, and a five foot length of kitchen aluminum foil cut into one inch squares. Simply place the bearings, the charcoal, and some of the aluminum in a small hobby rock tumbler. Continue adding the aluminum foil a little at a time and after a couple days they will grind into a fine powder. The steel bearings can be removed from the powder with a magnet and there you have German dark aluminum powder. If you have it available, ceramic media may be a better choice than steel ball bearings because ceramic can't produce sparks. This is not as big of a concern when making German dark aluminum powder as when you are making something like thermite. Some people advocate the use of a kitchen blender, spice grinder, or sander/bench grinder rather than a rock tumbler. The problem with a blender or grinder is that you will never get the consistency that a tumbler can produce, and you will likely destroy the blender. Also the blender/grinder method is violent and dusty and increases the risk of an unwanted fire. The same goes for vibratory polishers like the ones used in ammo reloading. Please note: if it weren't already obvious, German dark aluminum powder is highly flammable and thermite will liquefy solid steel while producing intense light that can damage unshielded eyes even a considerable distance away. Be careful!

The saboteur should never attack targets beyond his capacity or the capacity of his instruments. An inexperienced person should not, for example, attempt to use explosives or thermite, but should confine himself to the use of matches or other familiar tools. Explosives should rarely be encouraged as the potential of injuring the innocent should always be a consideration in every operation. Unrelated to fire or explosions, but in regards to safety, a cable under tension, like the support cables of a communications tower or any other cable under tension, can rebound with tremendous force when cut. Such a cable can move like a giant whip with enough force to cause unimaginable damage. For this reason, cutting support cables under tension should be strongly discouraged.

The saboteur should try to damage only objects and materials known to be in use by our enemy or to be destined for eventual use by our enemy. Without special knowledge, it may be undesirable for him to attempt destruction of food crops, food products, or public water supplies. After all, governments do a fine job of polluting those things without our help. Although the friend-saboteur may rarely have access to military or police objects, he should give these preference above all other targets, always keeping safety in mind.

(4-2) Immediately Prior to a Military or Militarized Police Action

Prior to a military/police offensive, during periods which are quiescent in a military sense, such emphasis as can be given to simple sabotage might well center on industrial and parts production, to disrupt the flow of materials and equipment to our enemy. Slashing a rubber tire on a police SUV may be an act of value; spoiling a batch of rubber in the production plant that is destine for a government tire contract is an act of still more value. While allowing substandard tires to be mass produced but with flaws that will cause more failures once installed may be the greatest value for the saboteur's investment. Now with understanding of this principle, the imagination of the individual industrial saboteur can take the idea beyond tires. Think about the array of computers and computer components in the modern police SUV. Each and every one of those components passes through hundreds of hands long before a coproach touches it.

(4-2.1)

GPS tracers and tracking devices placed on or in police vehicles could be helpful in many situations where friend-operatives need to know police routines and habits. Also it would be simple and inexpensive to modify an FM transmitter to constantly send a low power signal on a specific channel and permanently wire it into a police vehicle. Doing so would send an alert several blocks away when said vehicle approaches. The friend-operative could simply keep an FM radio turned on and set to the same frequency and whenever the police vehicle came within range the radio would blare the warning. This would be very handy if attached to SWAT vans.

(4-2.2)

Any communications facility which can be used by the authorities to transmit instructions or coordinate activities should be the object of simple sabotage. These include telephone, internet, power systems, radio, television, newspapers, and emergency broadcasting equipment including and especially emergency communication towers. The friend-saboteur should acquaint himself with the different types of communication towers and become familiar with the types used specifically for emergency and military communications. Many communication towers are powered by a simple power switch that, when thrown, essentially turns the tower off. Very often these switches are on the ground level of the tower in a separate little building behind a simple door lock. Sometimes the switch is located on the side of the tower secured by a simple pad lock. The friend-saboteur should learn the locations of these towers and, during non-emergency conditions, determine the security weaknesses and strengths of these facilities through extensive reconnaissance, and learn the weakness of the facility before the emergency arrives, so that at the right moment a strike can be made against the facility when it is needed the most by the authorities.

(4-3) During a Military or Militarized Police Action

The most significant sabotage for an area which is or is soon destined to be a theater of combat operations or concentrated police action, is that with which effects will be direct and immediate. Even if the effects are relatively minor and localized, this type of sabotage is to be preferred to activities whose effects, while widespread, are indirect and delayed.

The saboteur should be encouraged to strike transportation facilities and equipment, and communications equipment. Among such items are fueling stations, roads, automobiles, trucks, armored transports, police bicycles, and anything else used to transport State aggressors to the scene of their crimes, along with any form of communication they may use.

Critical materiel infrastructures, valuable in themselves or necessary to the efficient functioning of transportation and communication of the authorities during emergencies, also should become targets for the friend-saboteur. These may include oil supply lines, gasoline supply lines, natural gas supply lines, and sewer and water supply lines and treatment facilities. It may seem odd, but we have observed that authorities appear to understand the importance of protecting water supply facilities but apparently they don't understand the vulnerability of their sewage treatment facilities. During the onset of a large militarized police action a major failure of a sewage system on the other side of a city, preferably including a large sewage spill, has the potential of disrupting or distracting the police action.

5. SPECIFIC SUGGESTIONS FOR SIMPLE SABOTAGE

It will not be possible to evaluate the desirability of simple sabotage in every area without having in mind specifically what individual acts and results are embraced by the definition of simple sabotage. Therefore a listing of specific acts follows, classified according to types of target. This list is presented as an example rather than an exhaustive outline. As new techniques are developed, or new fields explored, it should be elaborated and expanded. For this reason feedback from those activists in the field is encouraged, as this information should be evaluated and included in future updates of this field manual.

Special Note on Explosives: With some exceptions, explosives are discouraged as a tool for the simple-saboteur for several reasons. First being the inherent danger of explosives to the saboteur. Second being the difficulty in preventing the innocent from being harmed. Third being the exaggerated response authoritarians exhibit when explosives are involved.

(5-1) Buildings

Government offices, court and municipal buildings, police stations, jails, county/parish utility maintenance buildings, and even corporate buildings of the Military-Industrial Complex or the Prison-Industrial Complex, along with obvious targets in the US like the NSA, FBI, BATF, DOJ, INS, IRS, DEA, DHS, TSA, FAA, etc., or their equivalent agencies in other governments are outstanding targets for simple sabotage. They are extremely susceptible to damage as will be listed below, and they offer some of the best opportunities to such friend-saboteurs as janitors, cleaning crews, and casual visitors; and when damaged, they present a relatively large handicap to our enemy both psychologically and actual.

(5-1.1) Fire

The use of fire is a point of controversy, but most will agree that if fire is to be used as a tool of simple sabotage it must be used selectively and with great care to avoid injuring the innocent or damaging private property. That said, fires can be started wherever there is an accumulation of inflammable material. Warehouses are obviously promising targets as are fuel storage areas, but incendiary sabotage need not be confined to them alone.

Whenever possible, arrange to have the fire start after you have left the area. Use a tea light and paper combination, setting it as close as possible to the inflammable material you want to burn. Remove the tea light from its metal base if it has one, leaving only the small candle. You may need to trim the edges of the candle to make it as small as is practical. This will leave as little residue as possible for inspectors to find after the fire. From a sheet of paper, tear a strip one or two inches wide and wrap it around the base of the candle two or three times. Twist more sheets of paper into loose ropes and place them around the base of the candle. When the candle flame reaches the encircling strip, it will be ignited and in turn will ignite the surrounding paper. The size, heat, and duration of the resulting flame will depend on how much paper you use. Additionally you may need to use a small amount of Vaseline or other petroleum jelly, on the strips of paper to help them ignite. Experiment with this process until you are comfortable and can repeat the results with each attempt before you use it for simple sabotage.

With a flame of this kind, do not attempt to ignite anything but easily inflammable materials. To light more resistant materials one could use such a candle as above plus tightly rolled or twisted paper which has been rubbed in more petroleum jelly. To create a briefer but even hotter flame, infuse dryer lint with petroleum jelly and form it into a nest of plain or saturated paper which is to be fired by a candle. Again, experimentation is the key to success.

To make another type of simple fuse, rub one end of a piece of cotton string with petroleum jelly. Rub a pinch of gunpowder over the inch of string where greasy string meets clean string. Then ignite the clean end of the string. It will burn slowly without a flame (in much the same way that a cigarette burns) until it reaches the grease and gunpowder; it will then flare up suddenly. The grease-treated string will then burn with a flame. The same effect may be achieved by using matches instead of the grease and gunpowder. Run the string over the match heads, taking care that the string is not pressed or knotted. This too will produce a sudden flame. The advantage of this type of fuse is that string burns at a set speed. You can time your fire by the length and thickness of the string you chose.

Use a fuse such as the ones suggested above to start a fire in an office after hours. The destruction of paper records and other types of documents can be a burden to the enemy. However fire may not destroy data on computers, so the impact may be more psychological than strategic. Once again, the selection of the target is key to achieving the maximum impact of the simple sabotage. Fire may be more useful as harassment or as a distraction than whatever it may accomplish on its own.

In basements or where waste material is kept, janitors should accumulate oily and greasy waste. Such waste sometimes ignites spontaneously, but it can easily be lit with a cigarette or match. If you are a janitor on night duty, you can be the first to report the fire, but don't report it too soon. Also a clean factory is not as susceptible to fire as a dirty one. Workers should be careless with refuse and janitors should be inefficient in cleaning and in handling flammable cleaning products. If enough debris and trash can be accumulated an otherwise fireproof building will become inflammable. Once again, fires can be timed with other events to draw authorities away from a more important activity.

(5-1.2) Water, Sewers, and Miscellaneous

Fire suppression or fire sprinkler systems may seem like the perfect way to commit simple sabotage. However automatic sprinkler systems vary in type, function, and design. Some types can be activated by simple means, others are complicated. Some systems spray water from all the sprinklers at once, others only activate one sprinkle at a time or one zone at a time. Some don't even use water. Some automatically contact the fire department, some don't. Some sound an audible alarm and some don't. Before you assume you can use a fire sprinkler system for sabotage find out the type of system used and make sure it will do what you expect it will do. Research is the key. Do your homework before you commit to a project.

Toilets and sewer systems are always vulnerable to a variety of simple sabotage, and unlike a fire, they are not likely to get out of control and cause unwanted damage or injuries. Every public building has toilet facilities and very little is done to protect them. Also it's reasonably safe to assume that restrooms are camera free zones. One plugged toilet won't close a building, but can be a source of irritation and frustration. However if the entire sewage system of a building can be disrupted, the building will need to be closed until the problem is resolved. A simple plug can be made with a large natural sponge. Moisten the sponge and squeeze it tightly into a ball, wrap it with string, and let it dry. Remove the string when fully dried. The sponge will be in the form of a tight hard ball. Drop it in a toilet and quickly flush it down. The sponge will gradually expand to its normal size and plug the sewage line. Some experimentation may be needed to get the right size sponge, but keep trying until you are successful. Expanding foam, sold at hardware stores in aerosol cans under the brand name "Great Stuff", can be used for more extensive sewer obstructions. Fill a small sandwich bag with the foam and quickly flush it down the toilet. The foam will expand and escape the bag, plugging the sewer line. Be careful, as the foam tends to stick to everything and won't wash off of hands and clothing. It may be possible to attach a longer tube to the nozzle of the can of foam and fish it down the toilet (3'-6'/1-2 meters) then discharge the foam directly into the sewer line. Such an action would take some planning and may involve leaving behind evidence, so always take that into consideration when planning any act of simple sabotage, especially those that involve D&D. Often times, outside of a building or in the basement or service area of the building, there are sewer cleanout access caps that can be easily opened and foam can be injected directly into the building's sewer service line.

Cans of expanding foam are difficult to conceal but can be used in an unending list of applications for clogging or gumming up the mechanical works of office machines, elevators, Heating/AC systems, and even security cameras. Quick shots of foam into computer case fans can slowly overheat computers. Expanding foam and injectable glues may be the perfect tools for the friend-saboteur, as their applications are only limited by the imagination of the anarchist.

Door locks and hinges are a weak point in the security of any building, but they can also be a source of irritation when they don't work correctly. Hardware and auto parts stores sell a product called "Loctite Threadlocker Red 271". This is an amazing product that comes in an easily concealable tube. With a quick squeeze, this product can be injected directly into locks or anywhere a key would fit. It quickly renders the lock useless. Hardware stores also sell a two part adhesive in a syringe, called epoxy. As you actuate the syringe the two parts mix into a hard powerful adhesive. Sometimes a toothpick or some other item must be used to stir the mixture for maximum hardening effect. You can use the syringe to inject the epoxy into the hinges of doors that are not in the viewing field of security cameras. This method can be used on older automobiles and trucks with manual door locks. It can also be used on windshield wiper arms and other locations. Your greatest weapon is always your imagination, so set it free to discover what mayhem you can bring upon our enemy.

In addition to all of the above, late night building maintenance workers can carefully switch signs and mislabel halls, floors, and rooms. Mislabel electrical panels and electrical switches or anything else that will cause low level confusion. Mislabel exits and entrances in parking garages. Move designated parking spaces to different locations, intentionally paint parking lines too close to each other, causing cars to be crammed together. Remove or alter overhead height/clearance warnings in parking garages. Building cleaning crews can randomly remove papers and reports from desks and unlocked drawers at night, or simply move items from one drawer to another or even from one cubical to another. Perhaps make it look like one cubical worker is stealing his coworker's items. Be selective with your targets and focus on the most productive State supporters and decision makers.

If you find it necessary to force entrance into a building, a window or door is usually assumed to be the best way to "break-in", however that may not be the case. Windows and doors are usually the primary location of security devices, cameras, and alarms. Interestingly enough, often the weakest point in a building is a ground level wall, preferably behind bushes or other landscaping. Many exterior walls are simple wooden frames, or studs set 16" to 24" apart, with thin "chicken-wire" and paper covered over with stucco. An inexpensive stud-finder will tell you where to avoid. Using any of several small hand tools, the stucco between the studs can be quickly and quietly compromised with light tapping and some prying, until the paper and wire can be cut away with pliers. The interior of these walls are often simple sheet rock that will also quickly and quietly break away with light tapping and prying.

(5-2) Travel and Transportation

(5-2.1) Railways and Airports

Make travel as inconvenient as possible for government supporters, media types, and military industrial complex management. Make mistakes in issuing tickets, leaving portions of the journey unconnected. If a government agent is trying to make a tight connection, create as many delays as possible. Over-book flights, cancel connections, then when the problems surface; slowly hand write customer complaints, ask an endless stream of questions, constantly apologize while doing nothing to solve the issue, prolong every process until the train/plane is nearly ready to leave or has left. Delete reservations, double charge those who are not paying attention, intentionally send them to the wrong airport or the wrong gate. Obtain access to the arrival/departure boards and randomly program small mistakes into the displays. See that the luggage of government supporters is mishandled or unloaded at the wrong locations. Switch address labels on baggage. Add confusing, suspicious, or embarrassing items into the luggage of government supporters. Be imaginative and have fun at the expense of those who seek to be our masters. Flyers for massage services, oversized adult toys, inappropriate pornography, receipts from strip clubs, or explicit love letters strategically placed in just the right baggage can be priceless to our cause. Always remember, these enemies of humanity would do far worse to you if they had half a chance, so show them no mercy.

(5-2.2) Automotive and Roads

Special Tip: Slicing a tire can be a quick down-and-dirty strike against authority. A nastier act is to use a razor knife set to a very shallow depth, not enough to go all the way through the sidewall of the tire, just enough to weaken it. (Use an old tire to practice getting the depth right.) Reach in to the interior side of the tire and make your slice from the metal wheel outward toward the tread. Your cut will not be visible, will not immediately cause a flat, and will likely blow when the vehicle is in motion. Because of the shape of the blowout it will likely appear as a manufacture defect or road damage.

For more fun, reprogram lighted signs to display nonsensical messages or false information. In areas where traffic is heavily composed of government autos, trucks, and convoys of various kinds, remove or change signs at intersections and on/off ramps of freeways. Remove or alter clearance signs on bridges and overpasses with low overhead clearance. Remove or alter weight limit signs on weak bridges. The removal of "DEAD END" and "NO OUTLET" signs can be very important before riots and demonstrations start as it becomes possible to bait heavy police/military vehicles into a situation where they can neither turn around nor escape. Always remember that locals know their streets and ignore signs, however in emergencies authorities move support from other areas and those outsiders rely upon signage. In Egypt rioters baited armored vehicles down narrow alleys then blocked the vehicles in with rubble, tractors, and construction equipment. Then they threw Molotov cocktails forcing the police to exit their vehicles and run away on foot.

More Special Tips: In spite of popular labeling of police vehicles as "tanks" or "Bearcats", the correct terminology is MRAP or Mine-Resistant Ambush Protected. In actual terms, that means nothing to us because we shouldn't be attempting to use mines, IEDs, or any other explosive device against police. But we should understand the inherent weaknesses of these vehicles. They are extremely heavy, roughly 36,000 pounds, which is almost magical for us when mud is involved. They have limited visibility and are difficult to maneuver on tight city streets and alley ways. A well placed Molotov cocktail at the base of the windshield will blind the driver. Some MRAPs have advanced optics, however many of these can be disrupted with fire since they are heat sensitive. Also, Molotov cocktails aimed at the running boards are far more effective than those aimed at the roof.

On the topic of Molotov cocktails, remember you are dealing with a tool that can quickly turn ugly. Before building, supplying, or using such a tool, ask yourself if you are willing to burn a man to death. Are you willing to cook a man alive? If not consider the alternative. A glue/glitter bomb may be able to disable the MRAR without the danger of killing the occupants or accidentally setting yourself on fire. The glitter bomb can be as easy to make as a Molotov cocktail while accomplishing the same task and far more humorous in execution. A simple balloon filled with a mixture of 50% Elmer's glue and 50% large glitter, carefully aimed at an MRAP windshield may have the same effect as a Molotov cocktail, that being the forced abandonment of the protection of the vehicle. However rather than burning the cop, we cover him with fabulous glitter much to the envy of stylish coproaches everywhere. After all, why kill when you can humiliate?

If you can initiate damage to a heavily traveled road, passing traffic and the elements will do the rest. If you have access to heavy equipment, use it to cut small ruts in asphalt roads; passing trucks will accentuate the ruts to a point where substantial repair will be needed. Newly paved highways can be easily damaged with a simple pickax. A few strikes in the new soft asphalt is all it takes to begin the process of destruction. This kind of sabotage is very important near capital cities, supporting the fact that governments are incapable of maintaining roads even for their own capitals. Once again, these activities should be done secretly so that when State supporters accuse us of sabotage the aboveground activists can accuse them of being paranoid conspiracy nuts. "As if anarchist have nothing better to do than go around digging pot holes in the middle of the night! Come on what next? Bigfoot masterminded 9/11? Crop circles are aliens sending anarchists coded signals?" This is the game they play with us, why not reverse it on them?

Taxi drivers can waste the enemy's time by driving slow, intentionally driving into congested areas, or by taking the longest possible route to the destination. When called for a pick-up take as long as possible to arrive. Create delays, make excuses, and pretend not to speak the language. Anything to delay and agitate the government supporter.

(5-2.3) Lodging, Hotels, and Motels

Front desk staff, food services, housekeeping, and building maintenance infiltration are extremely important in this sector of business. Travelers are at their peak of vulnerability, and typically have a high level of trust in the professionals in this industry. Friend-saboteurs who obtain positions in the hospitality industry should do all they can to keep their jobs and not be found out.

The list of simple sabotages available in the hospitality industry is only as limited as the individual imagination. Many of the same baggage handling sabotage suggested above under "(5-2.1) Railways and Airports", can be used here. 1) Two taxies are loading baggage at the same time, one guest is catching a flight at the airport the other is headed into the city for an extended business stay, and somehow the luggage gets blended. 2) The good reverend and his wife are in town to head up the congressional prayer breakfast and somehow a list of escort services appears in his bag along with a receipt dated from the last time the reverend visited the city without his wife. It has lipstick stains and the words; "Who's my favorite naughty sinner? Ask for Mercedes when you come back baby." 3) The four star general is in town to make an appearance on national television to answer questions about drone strikes on civilians in foreign countries and somehow three drops of phenolphthalein make it into his breakfast. A few hours later he rushes off camera and almost makes it to the men's room before he publicly soils himself. Oh, how embarrassing. Hopefully no one happened to be standing around with their cell phone in hand catching that for posterity. Side note of caution: phenolphthalein is very strong and will absorb through intact skin. Unless you want a case of screaming diarrhea, use caution when handling it, perhaps consider rubber gloves.

(5-3) Targeting Humans

Of all forms of simple sabotage, targeting humans may possibly turn out to be the most controversial practice, definitely the most dangerous, clearly requires the highest level of skill, and when done correctly is likely to be the most productive to our cause.

(5-3.1) The Media

The media have been the primary propaganda tool of the State. One can imagine five thousand years ago, a talented story teller garnering the king's favors by weaving a tail about how the king's mother may have been enticed and wooed by a tricky deity and that's why the king is so great, he is actually a half-god. And looking back one thousand years ago, what a catchy tune that troubadour is singing about the merciful king that forgives a criminal every year at the grand feast he throws for the poor. Then as now, governments steal the wealth of productive people and use it to brainwash those same productive people into loving the government that robs them. In the current manifestation of the State, news and entertainment are so intertwined that sometimes one wonders if it is even possible for the news media to fabricating a story so blatantly absurd that the general public would question its validity. And when a wildly inaccurate portrayal of news events is accepted as fact often the entertainment industry steps up with a major motion picture retelling the same lie, thereby reselling it to the gullible masses, including the ones who don't pay any attention to the news media in the first place. This presents a problem for those of us dedicated to the truth and committed to revealing that truth to as many people as possible. Our competition, the State puppets in the media/entertainment industry, are extremely well funded and well-motivated. Like the king's jesters, minstrels, and bards of old, they enjoy their spot near the royal banquette table and are always a part of the royal ball.

Trust in the media must be broken for us to succeed. The entire media con and all of its propaganda are like every other con job; it stands or falls on the rocks of trust. The phrase con job is short for "confidence job" because the only way a con job can work is if you have and take advantage of the confidence of the "mark" or victim. The moment the mark loses confidence in the con man, the con man loses the con. It therefore follows that if we are to beat the State's media puppets we must break the public's confidence in their version of current events and history. On the surface that would seem like an easy task. The media typically employs simple minded clowns who only seem to be talented in chattering a continual stream of nonsense fed to them in their earpiece. But in fact it is far more difficult than it seems.

You see, the relationship between the con man and the mark is not as simple as one might think. The mark wants to believe the con. Similarly the public wants desperately to believe the media/entertainment industry. Deep down inside the public knows that if they question the media and if the media is found to be lying, then they (the public) will be forced to do something. And the public hates it when they have to do something, especially if by "do something" we mean research the truth, weigh facts, learn new things, and then act on that newly found information. It's easier to just trust the guy with the perfect hair and gleaming smile that they watch every night on the magic talking box.

The key in defeating the media is the same key that must be used against the State on every field of conflict; that being to fight the enemy according to our strength and his weakness. To do this we must examine the strengths of the main stream media and entertainment complex and discover its weaknesses. We must avoid the temptation to fight the media on its choice of battlefield, and we must lure the media to our choice of battlefield.

In practical terms, as incredibly silly as it would be to invite the US military to an open battle, or as stupid as it would be to attempt something like an armed march on Washington DC, it is just as foolish to directly take on the main stream media by pouring money into our own media outlet designed to directly compete with NBC, CBS, CNN, Fox, BBC, etc., based around some dynamic personality or team of talented on-screen personalities. Liberty minded people who choose these kinds of foolish ventures should not be trusted in decision making since they clearly don't have the first bit of wisdom nor do they understand how competition in a State controlled market works. These ventures are tantamount to a person who plays on-line sword fight games taking on an actual sword master in a real fight with real swords.

The main stream media rely on the big production. The studio with the perfect lighting, the host with the perfect elocution, the seemingly informed experts on every imaginable topic, and the cutaway to the two minute thirty second video clip reinforcing what the talking head just explained.

This is not our battleground and these cannot be our weapons. On this battlefront, the aboveground activists can win the field, not by standing toe to toe with giants, but by an unending barrage of spit-balls fired from a million cynical straws poking out from behind every leaf. The aboveground activists must do what they do best. Mock authority, photo-bomb the man-on-the-street interview, laugh at the experts, pick every news cast apart on thousands of web sites, in short disrespect the mainstream media in every peaceful way possible. Use humor and parody to show the absurdity of the main stream media. Use inexpensive podcasts, cell phone footage, and live streaming content of actual events. Debunk the media and have fun doing it. Then, dear activists, leave the dangerous part to us, the underground.

(5-3.1.01) Deceive the deceivers

Recent history provides for us a hint of a massive inherent weakness of the main stream media. Adnan Hajj, a Lebanese freelance photographer, worked for Reuters for over ten years, supplying the news giant with at least 920 photos. In 2006 many of these obviously fake and altered photos were publicly exposed as such. It still took Reuters two years to purge them from its collection. Looking back on these old photos, it's amazing how bad the Photoshop work looks, and yet the media and the public believed them because they fit the narrative that Reuters was pushing.

On the topic of fitting the narrative, that brings us to the infamous Islamic Rage Boy, Shakeel Ahmad Bhat. Even if his name doesn't sound familiar you will almost certainly know his face if you were to see him. He has been used all over the main stream media and the alternative media as the poster boy of Islamic hate. And yet his personal story doesn't even begin to match his internet and media persona. But truth doesn't matter in an industry that sells lies. This is why the same old Palestinian woman, crying, pulling at her clothing, and sometimes pictured with a dead child, appears over and over in the media spanning ten years and portrayed in locations a thousand miles apart. Because she is an actor and the news is fake.

Still not convinced that the main stream media and its followers are gullible and given to overreact?

Consider the 2007 Boston Mooninite Panic. Such a stunt repeated in a different city every six months will both stimulate more rebellion to authority and drive the authoritarian stuffed shirts out of their tiny minds. In the case of the Boston Moominite Panic, almost everyone between the ages of 10 and 30 got the joke at the time, while almost everyone in government was aghast at this act of terrorism.

It's one thing to expose the main stream media lies or play up to their ignorance and fear. It's another thing to feed them lies intentionally to discredit them. Greed, prejudice, ignorance, and lust for attention drive the media. Their hunger for the outlandish causes them to accept any crazy lie so long as it serves their narrative. So we should feed them as much as they will swallow. Then step back and let our friends, the aboveground activists, expose their mistakes. The two pronged attack; we feed them fake news and our friends mock them for publishing it.

Would you care for some more down-and-dirty examples?

Learn the lesson of the Carlos Hoax from 1988, when a small lightly funded troop of merry hoaxters demonstrated for the world to see, that the main stream media were stupid, desperate, and gullible. Now, feed them fake news, fake pictures, fake reports, fake tips to the local and national media, as these are only the beginning. Disinformation during tragedies will humiliate the media, fake scandals on politicians, fake witnesses, hoax after hoax in a never ending barrage for as long as they will buy what we are selling. Friend-saboteurs should take acting classes and practice fooling the media. We can be crisis actors for freedom, getting on camera spinning incredible tails punctuated with a flood of tears. Expose local and national media as the buffoons and shrills of government that they are. Make throwies and mimic the Mooninite Panic. A throwie consists of a button battery, a diffused LED and a magnet taped together. Be creative. Tie Mylar balloons together, covered in LEDs, and release them as a fake UFO. Then call the media with UFO eye witness reports. Shark week may be over, but what about all the camel spiders that are invading the South West?

The opportunities are only limited by the imagination of the individual. The media constantly falls for the fake drug crazes that pop up from time to time, so feed them more of the same. So the "choking game" was a hoax, but what about all those kids getting high from "Ketchup LSD", made from fermenting ketchup and regular button mushrooms. (Fake! Not a real thing!)

Imagine the impact of a "news crew" that interviews a local police spokesperson about the success of the local school D.A.R.E. program, but unexpectedly asks the cop about local kids taking the Ketchup LSD. "Does your police office keep track of the children who have been admitted to the local hospital due to the Ketchup LSD fad?" "Do your D.A.R.E. officers warn the children about the deadly Ketchup LSD?" Now sit back and watch the pig squirm on camera. How about a call-in campaign to the local media about the growing problem in local hospitals with the Ketchup LSD fad? How many beds are occupied by these victims? In northern climates, the local news media may be vulnerable to fake school snow closing reports. What? An avalanche has engulfed the local Quickie Mart? Oh no! Apu Nahasapeemapetilon is dead!

Shall I go on? Do I really need to go on? You are only limited by your own mind.

(5-3.2) Psychological Operations

All successful warfare is based on deception. Hence, when we are able to attack, we must seem unable; when most active, we must appear inactive; when we are near, we must make the enemy feel safely out of our reach; when far away, we must haunt the dreams and the shadows of our enemy's mind and appear to be around every corner.

(5-3.2.1) Gas Lighting (Targeted Psych Ops as Simple Sabotage)

When several friend-saboteurs are working in the same location, be they coworkers, building maintenance, cleaning crews and janitorial staff, or any combination, you can work in harmony to disrupt the productivity of a target. Single out a specific target for your gas light operations. Use discretion in choosing your target. Look for someone who is actively involved in State aggression, a person highly productive in their field, but displaying signs of emotional stress, over-work, alcohol/drug issues, relationship issues, etc.. Take your time, observe his habits and look for weak points in his day to day routines.

Perhaps your target can become unstable by something as simple as moving his most used items from one place to another on a repetitive basis. Move his coat or sweater to the opposite side of his office or cubical. When he steps away for a cup of coffee or a restroom break, move his chair into his closet.

On a different day, remove one wheel from his computer desk chair and place it in his coat pocket. If he keeps his window blinds open, close them. Unplug his computer monitor while leaving everything else alone. Once your target begins to show signs of self-doubt, you can step up your operation. If you have ongoing direct visual with the target it may be possible to place very small wireless speakers in two or three locations in his work area. Control each speaker separately with your phone. Have five or six separate recordings of strangers saying his name. Alternate playing them, changing from one speaker to the next.

This process may seem cruel and heartless, but if your target's work directly facilitates the robbery, incarceration, torture, or death of the innocent then he has brought this on his own head when he entered such a field of endeavor. He should not be the recipient of our mercy if he makes his living from the suffering of the innocent.

(5-3.2.2) Hit Them Where They Live

Let's say you have developed a friend-saboteur network of five active friends all in the same general area. Let's say all of you have some outdoor or yard and garden tools, mowers, a wheelbarrow, a leaf blower, a small utility trailer, and a pickup truck. Or even better, one of your group owns a lawn service company. Let's say you have a target that is the subject of an active gas light operation in a near-by town. Let's say you do a little inventive printing and place fake company identifications on your truck and while the gas light subject's home is empty and everyone is at work or school, your crew of fake yard service workers remove or destroy the landscaping of his fine upscale home. Then send him a fictitious bill for the work. Then begin spoof-calling him from a fake bill collector.

Let's change that scenario slightly. Let's say none of your network of friend-saboteurs is talented in the ways of yard work, however one of your group owns an automotive towing and wrecker truck. Change the identification on your truck and when the subject goes to a store or other location where they will be away from their car for a few minutes, tow the subject's car to a no-parking area a few miles away and dump it there.

You say; "But none of my network of friends has a yard business or a tow truck." Well, that is the beauty of a distributed network with no central planner. Ask your friends what they have, what they can do, and make up your own plan.

(5-4) Identities

The Department of Homeland Security has revealed that during the 31 months from October, 2012, through April, 2015 more than 1,300 badges and credentials, 165 firearms, and 589 DHS cell phones were lost or stolen.

Having multiple identities is generally illegal. Using such identities in the commission of a crime multiplies the punishment that governments hand out to those who are caught and convicted. Skilled teams working with false identities can and have walked into prisons and walked out with prisoners. Having false identities can be a source of income for a subversive movement. Identities listed with the US Social Security Administration as being permanently disabled may receive monthly payments from the government of $1000 or more. Simple mathematics and logic tell us the US government hands a lot of money to a lot of accounts, and all of those can't possibly be legitimate.

One more note of caution in regards to identities: Do not simply jump on the dark net and grab the first fake identity someone is selling. It's far better for a member of the underground to develop the skill to produce false identities than to rely on a supplier of questionable motive.

(5-4.1)

The practice of hacking is intentionally not covered in this manual for a number of reasons, however this small word of encouragement is added for hackers and would-be hackers. Two types of hacking that require very little to no computer skills are often referred to as social hacking and visual hacking (some would place visual hacking as a subset of social hacking). Social hacking can include such things as the practice of getting people to let you in where you're not supposed to be, or to give you information they shouldn't. This is often done over the phone, but the skilled can do it in person. Visual hacking can include grabbing sensitive documents from an office printer or unattended desk, watching someone log into an account and remembering their login info, or searching through trash for private documents or personal information. The more a person practices social hacking the better he gets and eventually it becomes second nature to constantly be on the alert for opportunities to use your skills.

It shouldn't be necessary to explain how handy it is to have sensitive or personal information or access to private or secured locations, so we will simply add this; even if you don't know what to do with the information, someone in the friends network wants that information. Someone can use it.

(5-5) Forbidden Plants and Booze as Simple Sabotage

A wise man once said; "It is in war that the State really comes into its own: swelling in power, in number, in pride, in absolute dominion over the economy and the society." This is a true statement.

However it is in the trinity of prohibition, regulation, and taxation that the State owns the productivity of the individual, therefore facilitates war. When the State marries war with prohibition, regulation, and taxation, then we see the Beast stand to its full height.

The "War on Drugs" has been a ruse from the start, and only the simple minded or the intentionally-fooled ever believed it otherwise. It is an excuse to militarize the local police while using basic economics to create a Bogeyman (drug gangs/cartels/minorities) for the purpose of scaring and controlling the ignorant masses. The war on drugs provides the backdrop for rampant racism, as the prohibition is unequally prosecuted. At the same time, it's a method for funneling unimaginable amounts of undocumented cash into the pockets of select operatives in the intelligence community. In addition to all of the above, the alcohol industry and the incredibly powerful pharmaceutical industrial complex have long been supporters of the drug prohibition. When the time comes, governments will back down and allow more and more legal recreational drug usage. The move to "legalize it and tax it" and "legalize medical marijuana" are nothing more than a continuation of the same ruse, using pacification techniques to control public resistance. Eventually marijuana will become more mainstream and will be corporately controlled like the alcohol industry. Only a small handful of crony corporations will be allowed to grow it, transport it, or sell it. The price will be fixed by regulation, and taxation will be built into the price structure on multiple levels. That will not be a victory for freedom. It will be a successful act of pacification and neutering. Before then, during this window of opportunity, the drug war can provide several methods for simple sabotage.

Farmers, gardeners, and horticulturists can do a great service for our cause by hybridizing a strain of marijuana so that it reproduces faster and grows shorter in height. Activists can spread this weed on "public" land. Wooded areas of city parks, highway medians, fence rows, or anywhere that doesn't get mowed very often would be a great place to throw seed bombs. Imagine if marijuana grew rapidly and spread like dandelions. Now imagine trying to regulate or tax dandelions. If it's in great enough abundance the crony corporations won't be able to monopolize it and governments won't be able to eradicate it. But they will try. They will throw money, in crazy proportions, at a fight like this.

Much the same argument can be made for papaver somniferum, the opium poppy. This plant would be a beautiful addition to any flower garden, and few people would have any idea its purpose. Imagine if some industrious gardener were to start heavily producing seeds for seed bombs. Much of California and the western mountain states have a very similar climate to Afghanistan and Turkey where it grows and viciously self-seeds. The gardener that did this service to our cause would be a true saboteur.

Hooch, moonshine, white lightening, white liquor, or any other name you want to use, can be safely produced on a countertop with a device not much bigger than a coffee maker, for a fraction of the cost of corporate alcohol. Current to the writing of this manual, a counter top device like described above is being sold by several independent manufactures on the internet for about $200, and can consistently produce a safe, decent quality vodka for about $5 per gallon. Now tell me about growing your tomato garden for agorism. Why is any anarchist buying government liquor?

Like Bitcoin, agorism in the production of forbidden or restricted products like these undermines the authority of the State, creates funding for more projects, and stimulates the black market economy.

So what are you waiting for? Super glue that cops wiper blades, glitter bomb that mayor, and let's all throw our shoes into the gears of this machine until it grinds to a halt!

More ideas? Okay, how about these for future chapters:

- Baiting politicians, judges, and police chiefs into honeytraps for extortion, profit, and fun!
- Developing a transportation network to move activists and dissidents away from government reach and into safer areas.
- Use of drop phones
- Use of VOIP
- Use of VPN
- Use of TOR

Do you like these ideas? Great, write the chapters and add them to this book.

To The First Lego Brigade

Friends,
Be safe, have fun, do your best, and be proud of what you do.

END: Part 2 SIMPLE SABOTAGE

Part 3 ETHICS BASED SELECTIVE IRREGULAR WARFARE

To Governor William Tryon, and all such tyrants:

WHEREAS it has become apparent to the citizens of Bavarian Gulch, that there is no security for life and property, either under the regulations of society as it at present exists, or under the so-called law as now administered; Therefore we, whose names are hereunto attached, do unite themselves into an association for the maintenance of the peace and good order of society, and the preservation of the lives and property of the people of Bavarian Gulch, and do bind ourselves, each unto the other, to do and perform every lawful act for the maintenance of true natural law and order, and to sustain those laws when faithfully and properly administered; but we are determined that no thief, highwayman, politician, banker, or murderer, shall escape punishment, either by the quibbles of the so-called law, the insincerity of persons, the carelessness or corruption of the police, or a laxity of those who pretend to administer justice.

Harmon Husband V
John V Brown
John Wilkes
Nat V Kinney
The unanimous declaration of agreement by The Remaining Elders of The Baldknobbers represented herein by this mark: XX

1. ETHICS-BASED IRREGULAR WARFARE DEFINED

In the first section of this manual titled Peaceful Sedition, a set of definitions was presented explaining some of the wording used in this manual. Since this section of this manual is specifically dealing with ethics-based irregular warfare, the writers of this section have chosen to use that stated definition and expand on it slightly.

Irregular warfare favors indirect and asymmetric approaches, so we will begin by establishing exactly what we mean by indirect and asymmetric. An open and direct confrontation with an enemy who possesses dramatically superior resources is never wise and is usually suicidal. Therefore we must prefer small hit-and-move confrontations where we almost never fight an extended battle and we almost never confront more than one or two opponents at a time. Whenever possible, we should outnumber our opponents by a factor of 2:1 or even 3:1. There are exceptions to this, for example when a well-hidden rifleman can strike a high value target and safely extract himself from the engagement he could do so without a number advantage. Likewise, we must never attempt to hold or capture a geographic location of any kind, but we must remain fluid so that at any moment's notice we can disperse into the vastness of the human tide. If possible, every confrontation should be planned and should be initiated on our terms. Targets should be carefully selected based on their priority and their vulnerability. Hard targets should be avoided at almost any cost. Our purpose and focus should always be on the long victory and we must never allow short sighted goals or temporary gains to lure us into believing that this war can be won by military means. Our primary purpose is to agitate and irritate our enemy, not defeat him. In a way, we are simply here to whip the money changers and knock over the tables. Our purpose is not to confront the might of the legions nor defeat the empire. The market will defeat the State. Our job is to erode our adversary's power, influence, and the individual's will to fight, while economics and the aboveground activists do the job of shifting market demand. Through self-discipline and mutual encouragement we must maintain this style of fighting until the true powers behind the throne reveal themselves and become vulnerable. Then and only then we must shift our focus and descend upon them with single-minded dedication to decapitate the State through direct strikes against the true leadership. When that day comes we must show no mercy, we must wear the edges off the guillotines and run the wood chipper's fuel tanks dry.

The thing that differentiates our version of irregular warfare from terrorism and other government supported guerrilla fighting is that we must always maintain the moral high ground by insisting all of our actions be ethics based. In other words; no matter the outcome, our actions themselves must fall within the limits of property rights and defense as outlined elsewhere in this manual. Unlike our enemy, we must never strike the innocent for the purpose of "moving the herd". We must never intentionally cause fear in the hearts of the innocent, and we must never intentionally sacrifice an innocent life for our cause. Our targets must always be specifically chosen, and not the result of chance. Our strikes must be with precision causing as little risk to bystanders as possible, for that reason we should avoid using explosives as weapons, as much as reasonably possible. And finally every action must be for the purpose of disrupting the State, not to bring glory or recognition to any individual nor even to the cause itself.

(1-1) Stomping Sand Castles

We shall not grow wiser
Until we learn that much of what we have done
Was very foolish

We wish it were not necessary to write this manual. We wish the bulk of humanity would not have allowed itself to become content in its own captivity, while forcing that captivity upon the rest of us. We wish those talented in the ways of self-defense and endowed with the independent warrior spirit had stood up and crushed the State and its supporters before the State had the opportunity to systematically dumb them down to the point that so few are left that can still think and fight. But we also know that no matter what each of us may wish, the reality of the situation is that a war is coming, and we can choose to fight it on our terms or we can suffer the consequences of allowing the Enemy of humanity to choose those terms and place this war upon us. Knowing that only the fool and the desperate fight on their enemy's terms, we choose to be neither the fool nor the desperate. We choose to plan, we choose to prepare, we choose to learn, and we choose to fight on our terms and on our schedule.

Unfortunately a portion of this manual must be dedicated to correcting the mislead, reprimanding the arrogant, and mocking the foolish. Before we can show you how to arm yourself and how to fight a winning war, we must first destroy those precious sand castles that so many have spent so much time and resources building. It would be nice if we had the talent, the time, and the media outlets to carefully walk everyone though this process without offending anyone, while at the same time being entertaining and making everyone feel good about themselves. But we don't have that luxury, and neither do you. We have serious business ahead of us and we need to clear out of our ranks those who can't handle the challenges that are coming towards us at an alarming speed. Preconceived notions, pride, machismo, and ego need to be set aside and a realistic understanding of our resources, our strengths, our weaknesses, and our character need to be examined. Then you need to ask yourself if you are suited to step up and accept this challenge, or if you would prefer to adjust your chains and go back to enjoying government bread and circuses while passing the State on to your children.

At least one of the sand castles that we will be stomping will be American-centric, however we will try to make this presentation broad enough that non-Americans can still find it useful. To clarify what is meant by that, too many Americans simply don't think of the rest of the world as even existing when they think about things like police brutality, property confiscations, and other forms of tyranny. When they think of the State, they only think of the DC government, rather than the bigger picture of the State as described in this manual. Somehow they have developed the mentality that Washington DC is the center of their problem, and if a few politicians in that city were subdued or replaced then we would all live on the Big Rock Candy Mountain where gum drops grow on lollipop trees and trained monkeys ride unicorns delivering ice cream sandwiches to all the happy children. Many Americans ignore other governments around the world that are every bit as evil as DC, and that would be more than happy to rush in to fill any power vacuum that would develop if DC fell. They also tend to ignore the fact that governments around the world oppress the local populations, often times with the aid of the DC government, and incredible numbers of people are ready to stand up to their governments today, they just lack the knowledge of how to do it successfully.

Many Americans don't understand that to be successful the march to freedom must be a worldwide action by the friends of freedom in every land. We must tear down this Beast everywhere he resides. We must give him no quarter and he must find no sanctuary. Once this process begins and as long as the fight for freedom continues we cannot rest and we cannot let our enemy hide and regroup behind the borders that politicians have drawn on maps.

Many Americans often ignore the local government employees that both enforce the will of DC, while also daily enforcing the will of local tyrants, drunk with power and hungry for glory. These same types of Americans often idolize the American military, made up of some 1.3 million of their own families and neighbors that carry out the orders of the DC government. Many willfully forget that when the DC government sends its Hellfire missiles to murder in faraway lands and sends its agents to rape and torture in hidden camps around the world, those Hellfire missiles are guided by young men and women taken right out of American high schools and universities in their own neighborhoods, and those US government agents who crushed the testicles of a small boy to punish his father are also recruited right out of the local American schools. These Americans who often hate the DC government, choose not to realize that the most evil things that a government does happen because someone they know obeys orders, and most often does so on a local basis. Often these patriotic Americans deeply believe that their precious American military will stand with them and protect them from the DC government, ignoring the countless lessons from history that prove the exact opposite. They choose not to realize that their cousins and their neighbors, whether wearing the uniform of the DC legions, their state's National Guard, or the uniform of the local police, have been trained and conditioned to not only obey orders but to believe they are doing so for the greater good.

This is why 19 year old Ohio National Guardsmen were able to take aim and kill 19 year old Kent State students in Ohio on May 4, 1970, and this is how Massachusetts National Guardsmen were able to go house to house aiming automatic rifles at old people and children in Watertown Massachusetts on April 19, 2013 under the guise of a search for a teenager that, at the time, was only suspected of a crime.

This is how a church in Waco Texas was burned to the ground on April 19, 1993, while children were contorting in pain from the chemicals being pumped into their storm shelter. And this is how American soldiers of the 12th Infantry Regiment and the 3rd Cavalry Regiment, commanded by Douglas MacArthur, and supported by battle tanks commanded by George Patton, attacked and murdered retired and disabled American veterans and their families in Washington DC on July 28, 1932. The sand castle idea that when times turn bad, the US military will disobey orders and come to the aid of the people of America is delusional at best, and extremely dangerous under any circumstances. Those of us with our eyes open should avoid any kind of reliance upon people who insist upon believing such ridiculous myths and fantasies.

Another sand castle that needs to be stomped into the dirt is the notion that at some undeterminable point in the future, the DC government will cross an imagined, completely undefined "line-in-the-sand" and brave patriots will rally around the flag and restore the republic. If you once believed this at some time in the past don't feel bad, many of us have been fooled. If you still believe this nonsense today, stop reading this manual now and seek to educate yourself on the nature of the State, because you are not mentally equipped for this fight.

First, the DC government didn't suddenly turn bad. It was the bastard child of evil from the day it was conceived in the twisted minds of Hamilton, Washington, John Jay, Henry Knox, and other founding members of The Society of the Cincinnati. It was planned from its conception to eventually be a totalitarian government, and with the exception of a few stumbles along the way, it has faithfully followed that path ever since. Additionally, this process was clearly warned against and predicted at the time of the "founders" by the writers of the Anti-Federalist Papers. In other words, the American government you see today is exactly what its designers wanted when they designed it, and the excuses given by American "patriots" not to burn it to the ground today are the same weak excuses they gave at every stage of its development since 1787. The Constitution of the United States of America was and is a document of enslavement intended to fool the weak minded while pacifying those who possess the moral fortitude and intelligence to stand up to tyranny.

Second, if there actually was a magic "line-in-the-sand" it was crossed long before anyone reading this manual was born, and no one has risen up yet. Third and finally, the idea of patriots rising up is usually tied to the idea that another revolution is the answer to our problem. This is false because revolution, by definition, is simply a turning around to arrive where we started, and we don't need to start this tyrannical process over again, we need to kill it once and forever.

The next sand castle that needs to be kicked into the air and scattered into the wind, is the crazy notion that large sections of America, or perhaps states like Texas, Alaska, or New Hampshire, can break away or secede from the DC government and freedom will somehow abound. Set aside the obvious problem of the afore-mentioned 1.3 million federal troops, the strongest army the world has ever seen, in the hands of the DC government, along with the ability and motivation to send death from the sky to visit every rebel state house, VFW lodge, and back yard BBQ where the "terrorist rebels" gather, and the idea becomes laughable at best. But add into the equation that the very idea of establishing a "free state" is self-contradictory. Then consider the contradiction of having a "free" society with government established borders, and you enter the realm of collectivist hallucinatory delusions. Secession is the path to open geography-based war, the one type of warfare Washington DC actually knows how to win. These notions of state secession are generally pushed by "leaders" who fantasize of being the next "father of their country" and would lead their followers right back into tyranny once the irresistible temptations of power take their natural course, assuming the DC government doesn't just round them up and exterminate them wholesale. Secession and revolution are the battleground the DC government is best suited for and clamors to fight. Give them that fight and you secure their tyranny for generations to come.

If you haven't already noticed, this manual is not written as a gentle persuasion to nudge you toward freedom. It's a hard primer to snap fresh troops into action so that they may stay alive, yet having the greatest possible impact against our enemy while remaining within the confines of the Zero Aggression Principle. This manual is not all encompassing, it is not an exhaustive text book, it is not the definitive authority on anything, and it should only be an introduction to irregular warfare.

In reality this manual is nothing more than a drill instructor, in your face screaming his lungs out so that you will not do something stupid that gets you or others like you killed. This manual is the glass of ice water down the back of your neck, to wake you up from the hypnotic stupor your "liberty leaders" have seduced you into. This war is ours to win if we do it right, or ours to lose if we refuse to use wisdom, or fail to keep our actions ethical. As much as the soft-world wants you to compromise, get along, and unite, you must stand on principles, inflict justice, and scatter the collective into the dusts of history, otherwise you should return to the cotton fields and keep your head bowed low until the master decides he will let you have an extra chicken.

Let's just pause and recap these points, as they are the cornerstone of this part of this manual and cannot be overemphasized. Washington DC, although a disgusting swamp of corruption and tyranny, is not alone in its crimes. Local tyrants and their servants enable the federal government to be what it is and absent the federal overlords, those locals would become just as bad as or worse than their DC masters. The myth that the US military will come to the aid of the American people is counterfactual and a deadly mythology that history has disproven. Outside of the political borders of America lies a world on the verge of meaningless revolution, that can be redirected to join us in a meaningful war against the true enemy of humanity, the State. But we must realize there is no magic line-in-the-sand somewhere in the future. Slavery is upon us now unless we stand up and free ourselves. We can fight the war our grandfathers failed to fight or we can pass this slavery on to our grandchildren and accept the scorn we rightfully deserve. We must never accept the morphine of half measures, nor settle for a slightly more comfortable slavery under a local master. And we must not be baited into open confrontation with the strongest military the world has ever known, fighting an old style geography-based conventional war. We must never attempt to take or hold a physical location or geographic area. We must never let our enemy decide the battlefield. Not even once. We must fight unseen, undetected, without glory or recognition for our victories and without sympathy for our losses. We must punch the enemy where he doesn't expect it and move before he can react. This is how we fight this Beast and this is how we kill him.

The final sand castle to be crushed is the so called "castle doctrine", perhaps the most precious castle in western culture. Since pre-Roman times, a man's house was his castle, a place no tyrant or his lieutenants had the right to enter without permission. Even the vampires of European myth and legend could not breach the door posts uninvited. This foundational property right was the basis of our conception of privacy and the idea that government agents needed a warrant to enter our homes. In today's world, the castle doctrine, no matter the platitudes, is de facto-dead. If you, the individual, are brave or foolish enough to exert your right to protect your home and regulate who enters and under what circumstances that entry takes place, you may enter the land of the dead on the express train as SWAT teams cut you down, or unmanned unseen aircraft rain death on you from above. A right ceases to be a right if it is impossible to enforce. If that sentence offends your sense of good and bad, then good for you; there is hope for you. Currently this right of property is dead, but there are those of us who will see it resurrected. But before we can do so we must first remove the power that has crushed property rights at every turn. We must kill the State, and the State lives so long as its enforcers and benefactors live. Therefore seeing that we have been systematically attacked, we must defend ourselves and our property by killing the threat and those presenting said threat. But we cannot do it standing in our doorways. That battle ground has been lost and we must fall back and proverbially "head for the hills" where our safety has always been. We must shift the battlefield to our advantage and become a fluid force that cannot be detected, cannot be pinned down, and cannot be defeated. The individual warrior must embrace ethics-based irregular warfare and learn the lesson of Buppert's Law, roughly stated; "A mountainous people with a rifle culture cannot be defeated by conventional forces." That said, in many cases the individual warrior may not have access to actual mountains for refuge, therefore many will have to adapt their methods according to circumstances.

However it is the opinion of the authors of this manual that a rifle culture is imperative to our victory.

Keep in mind that in February 2013 former Los Angeles coproach Christopher Dorner, one lone actor proficient with a rifle, froze the entire "law" enforcement complex in southern California in fear for nearly a month. One severely disturbed man had that kind of an impact with no support network and a horribly flawed approach and method. Consider what he could have done with a clear mind, a solid philosophy, a dependable partner, a network of sympathizers, and if he had not confined himself geographically.

We have both the moral high ground and the logistics on our side if we fight an extended series of individual battles using wisdom and a disciplined ethics-based irregular warfare approach. We have found ourselves in this position, not because we chose to be aggressed upon, but because we choose to stop the aggressor.

2. CAMOUFLAGE IS NOT A FASHION STATEMENT

He is skillful in attack when his enemy does not know what to defend
He is skillful in defense when his enemy does not know what to attack

To the mall ninja, to the barroom hero, to the monster truck aficionado, to the connoisseur of low calorie beer, and to the fly fishing jig expert, camouflage is a fashion staple. To the individual warrior, camouflage should not be synonymous with Woodland, Tiger Stripe, MultiCam, or TACAM. Camouflage should rather be a word synonymous with phrases like; fitting in, hide in plain sight, and "Honest officer I didn't see anything or anyone unusual."

Our enemy, the State, has the luxury of fighting wars of attrition. He has an endless supply of servants to call upon to pour into fields and down roads to their deaths. He adorns them in impressive uniforms and teaches them to march in ridiculous unnatural ways so that everyone can see how blindly and fanatically they serve him. He teaches them to snap their heads from side to side, exaggerate their steps, and swing their arms like broken windmills. And they obey. No matter what absurd costumes the State requires, big furry hats, fringe covered shoulders, or colorful sparkly insignia, servants of the State strut themselves about showing their fervor for service, while proudly whoring their dignity to their master. Watching a military parade should immediately put one in mind of the Paris fashion runways where pathetic brainless drones don ridiculous costumes and march about with a dead look in their eye for the perverted pleasure of a small group of rich women. Except in the case of the military parades, the brainless drones in costume kill on command and throw away their own lives for their rich political masters. And unlike those of the fashion models, the families of the military slaves take great pride when their sons and daughters die senselessly over a stretch of sand or a bombed out hill. Or worse yet, the broken slaves, no longer useful to the politicians, come home with war ravished bodies and minds and are relegated to live out their miserable existence in homeless shelters or under a bridge near a trash dumpster where they can find some morsel to eat. Even in this shameful condition the burned-out souls will often continue wearing some tattered camo painted remnant of their costume. This is how the State treats its most faithful slaves. And thus we see our enemies; not the broken slaves, but the men and women who use the State to destroy lives, including destroying their own slaves.

We must not use people like this, nor should we allow ourselves to be used like this. The individual warrior is a rare commodity that must be respected and cherished. If victory is to be obtained it will be through each individual warrior realizing that his or her strength doesn't lie in the collective power of waves of dead soldiers, but in the success of staying alive, of moving without being observed, and of striking and vanishing without being remembered. This is the power of camouflage. To appear so much a part of the scenery that no one notices that you are there and then no one notices when you leave. In modern first world irregular warfare this is not done by breaking light and shadow patterns and mimicking leaves or grass. It's done by looking and acting like you should be where you are.

We will stay alive and we will defeat the State only when we pick our battle, when we strike where the enemy is not guarding, and when we present our enemy with no way to strike us back. In frustration, the State will punish the innocent, and that will create even more of us to strike him again. With more careful strikes against the State, the State will commit more resources to swinging at our shadows. Simple mathematics teaches us that a single bullet only costs us a few small coins, but governments must respond with mountains of cash and dramatic oppression of the innocent. As that oppression rises, faith in the State shrinks. This is our part in the process that leads to the death of our enemy, the State.

3. JUSTIFICATION AND TARGET ACQUISITION

They who employ force by proxy are as much responsible for that force as though they employed it themselves.
Herbert Spencer

If you're reading this then it shouldn't be necessary to go to great lengths or to spend a lot of energy convincing you that preemptive self-defense is always the wisest form of self-defense. Also it shouldn't be necessary to justify the concept of engaging in irregular warfare with proven aggressors like individual violent police, specific decision makers, or military actors who follow orders and kill on command, but the difficult thing about government is that by its very design it's a massive structure created to shift the blame to so many hands that no one can be held responsible. This collectivist notion is perhaps best displayed in the story of the death of Julius Caesar, where each senator took a turn stabbing Caesar so than no one person could be guilty of the assassination. Of course that only works as a collectivist argument. The moment you introduce individual accountability the collectivist argument vanishes like a shadow in sun light.

So how do we determine the level of responsibility of each statist, and how do we determine what our response to each of those statists should be once we accept our role as individual warriors engaging in irregular warfare?

That can be a question of extreme complexity if we allow it to be, but it's simply not necessary to allow it to be complex if we narrow our fight to targets where no question is present. In other words, don't allow yourself to be caught up in such a target rich environment that you fail to see the obvious shots. Think of the lion in the field with a thousand gazelle. Once he reveals himself they will all bolt, and his field of vision will be filled with moving shapes and bouncing targets. The wise lion doesn't just go for whichever gazelle jumps, because the moment they run none of them will be catchable. The wise lion picks out one easy shot. He takes his time. He prepares. He knows a wasted attempt is wasted energy, and he knows he can't afford wasted energy. Failed hunts mean starvation. So he fixes his eyes on one target, and when the moment happens he refuses to be distracted. For the individual warrior the State provides such a target rich environment that it's easy to be distracted. It's easy to chase philosophical rabbits down never ending rabbit holes, debating about which cops are good and which are bad, and if the mailman is robbing you through taxation, and if the parking enforcement officer has crossed some line; or you can stop, clear your mind, focus, and do your job. There are plenty of violent cops with incredibly horrible records, who have been documented and filmed beating homeless people for no reason, and killing anyone who crosses them, and there are plenty of bureaucrats enabling and protecting those violent cops. We don't need to attack a collective any more than we need to be distracted by that collective. We need to carefully do our homework, review our decisions with a verifiable process, and take the needed actions to secure our freedom. As we pick the fruit that is ripe, the tree will see to it that more fruit ripens in its time.

(3-1) Pause and Review

Let's pause for a moment and review a line you just read: We need to; (1) carefully do our homework, (2) review our decisions with a verifiable process, and (3) take the needed actions to secure our freedom. These three points are critical.

(3-1.1) Do Your Homework

The first thing to keep in mind is that we are not concerned about justifying our actions to a government court. If it comes to that we are sunk. In the minds of the statists, we're already criminals just for discussing these things, much more so for acting on them. Our concern should primarily be; what is right and what is wrong. This is why the statement was made earlier that we should concentrate on picking the fruit that is ripe. We shouldn't take action against any target where there is doubt of guilt. We should take our time, research accusations, and be slow to make our judgment. The exception being a situation where time is pressing and the target is actively a serious threat to the innocent. But under normal circumstances, where we have time to rely on the investigative process, the individual warriors can work with trusted non-combatant members of the underground. Activity like gathering video evidence of crimes, hacking personal files, gathering of private data like addresses, shopping habits, and any other information that will help the underground build a fair and honest profile of the accused target and the activities in his private life, would be tremendously helpful. This process is especially important for the less obvious targets like bureaucrats, key corporate enablers, and even drone operators who do their murdering behind the cloak of government secrecy.

(3-1.2) Review Decisions with a Verifiable Process

Again, assuming the target is not an immediate and serious threat to the innocent, then we can consider two options; the first being the best practice, and the second being a less desirable practice that should only be used when absolutely necessary.

The best practice would be a reviewable collecting and documenting of the accusations followed by a specific stating of the charges, then followed by a review by at least three reliable parties, finally either a unanimous decision of the three reliable parties, or a delay until a unanimous decision can be agreed upon. If a unanimous decision is not directly forthcoming, that target should be dropped from consideration and the next target up for review should be considered.

This process could be done both privately and secretly, while the overall process can be recorded in the Bitcoin blockchain for later review and public scrutiny. It would cost a very small amount of Bitcoin to make a transaction with an encrypted transcript imbedded in the transaction, so that after the fact if the results of the "trial" needed to be reviewed, the encryption key could be released or even shared on a need-to-know basis, and either opened to the public or it could remain locked if no one challenged the trial or the process.

The less desirable practice would be a direct private conversation between two or three individual warriors working together as a team, and if an agreement is made as to the target's guilt, then the team does what they need to do. Circumstances my dictate that this process is the only one available. That would be unfortunate, but sometimes a perfect world is simply not available.

(3-1.3) Taking Action

In a perfect world, we would make our strike as the target is attacking a victim. A public display such as this could work in our favor, but if botched or if there is some public question as to the guilt of the target, then this could become a publicity nightmare. Also if you consider the structure of the State, the obvious killers wear police uniforms and usually only kill one at a time, but the real murderers in government kill dozens or even thousands with a few words or the stroke of a pen on paper. The best practice is a quiet, preferably private situation when the target is alone and it can be made to look like an accident or a suicide, or the target can simply vanish. The longer the individual warriors are working without being seen or even suspected of existing, the better we are doing our job. In this process we can take a lesson from the CIA and other such crime syndicates that operate in the shadows.

Always remember, we are not in this for the gore or the glory. We're in this to free the world of those who relish in gore and glory. We must always guard that we don't become what we fight. One method that may be helpful would be for a strike team to come together for a specific job, within a specific timeframe, then once the event is done the team could disband and return to normal life, with no team contact until a preset time. With enough teams working in rotation, the burden of such actions can be lightened and it can be harder for our enemy to discover the functioning of our networks.

(3-2) Target Acquisition

Those that are generally thought of as the powerful in the world are the politicians, but this is part of the illusion of government. When we look at politicians, we are as it were, looking at the grass on a hill. The grass is not the hill, and in fact the grass adds very little to the hill. But it's what we see. Like grass, politicians are seasonal. They sprout up quickly, put on a show and then vanish into the soil, their demise bringing life to the next seasonal explosion of drama, as the new generation of politicians reach for the sky. Politicians hold a temporary but obvious position that, no matter how it appears, has very little power. If you dig deeper into the hill you find the grass is rooted in the soil and the soil provides the nutrients that determine if the grass lives or dies. The soil is critical to the dramatic performance of the grass, so in that sense the soil, or better stated, the dirt in our metaphorical hill is the massive network of unelected bureaucrats, party bosses, lobbyists, and the permanent understructure of men and women that do the actual running of the day to day functions of government. The grass comes and goes, but bureaucracy stays. These people, the dirt of governments, do the actual developing of the policies and laws, they hand down the regulations, they introduce the politicians to the right lobbyist, to the right donor, and to the right power people in corporations and banks. These people determine when, where, and how tall the grass grows. And yet, the dirt is not the hill. The hill is in reality the rocks that thrust up from the valley floor. The corporate giants and the banking cartels are the rocks that are almost unmovable. The rocks determine if there is or is not a hill. The rocks are the true power. Everything else is on the surface protecting the rocks from exposure to the elements. So long as the rocks remain covered they don't erode and the hill lives on. Take away the dirt and the grass vanishes and the rocks begin to crumble and weather away.

If politicians are like the grass on a hill, police are like the annoying insects that crawl all over the surface of that hill. Watching a video of a violent cop beating a pregnant woman, kicking her stomach and stomping on her face, should infuriate any sensible person. Seeing the video of the handicapped man in Florida handcuffed to a wheelchair while police walk by and casually pepper spray his face until he asphyxiates and dies, should be a source of outrage and should make anyone want to act against these brutal murderers. Studying the case of Kelly Thomas, the disabled man beaten to death by Manuel Ramos, Jay Cicinelli, and Joseph Wolfe who wore the uniforms of the Fullerton California Police Department on the night of July 5, 2011, should fill your heart with both pity and rage. But the uncomfortable fact of the situation is that if there were a magic trigger we could pull that would cause every single violent murderous cop in the world to suddenly drop dead, the actual power brokers of the State would hardly blink, as they simply hired another hive of violent ego-driven hate-filled idiots to replace the dead ones. Unfortunately there is an endless sea of angry morons who would just love to have a legal excuse to beat weak people while wearing a uniform and collecting a fat pay-check. So as temporarily gratifying as it may be, simply pulling that magic trigger on a world of violent cops won't stop the process that makes them. It does little more than crushing a few ants to stop an infestation.

That's not to say that given the opportunity to stop them, murderous scum should be allowed to continue their rampage upon the defenseless. Stopping the senseless beatings and killings of the innocent is one job of the individual warrior, assuming he can do so safely without exposing himself or his network. But the better target is the police chief who places the violent cop in that position and then publicly defends him when he does his evil deeds. Yet a better target still is the politician who appoints that chief, or the even higher power broker who uses his influence to say who the next mayor, senator, or president will be. The deeper you dig into the darkness the more important and more difficult the target becomes. So violent dangerous police are easy targets that deserve our attention. But dealing with them won't solve our problem. As much as we would like to spend our time crushing bugs, those bugs are simply a symptom of the problem of the hill. We must expose the rock so that the forces of nature can follow its course.

One thing to keep in mind is that evil doesn't look the way the State has taught you to expect evil to appear. When you look through the eyepiece of a scope you will not find Adolf Hitler or Hannibal Lecter. You will find someone who looks very much like you. You won't see that person as he or she kicks in a door or throws a flash-bang in the crib of a baby, you won't see them as they torture and torment a prisoner, and you won't see them as they authorize a Hellfire missile strike on a family during a wedding. You will be more likely to see them as they sit in traffic listening to morning radio or as they open their mail box. This is the reason fighting and killing the State is so difficult. Because it usually doesn't appear as it really is. The people who are most important to keeping the State alive are the ones we have almost no chance of reaching. And most of the ones we can easily reach don't really matter to the continuation of the State. Other than the untouchable few at the tops of the banking cartels and corporate consortiums that make the State possible, the most important targets that can actually make an impact in this war are the people referred to by Michael Glennon in "National Security and Double Government" as the Trumanite network. According to Glennon:

"...Trumanites can have no real discussions with family or friends about work because nearly all of their work is classified. They hold multiple compartmented clearances. Their offices are located in the buildings' expensive real estate-the Pentagon's E-Ring, the CIA's Seventh Floor, the State Department's Seventh Floor. Key pads lock their doors. Next to their desks are a safe and two computers, one unclassified and the other classified. Down the hall is a SCIF167 where the most sensitive briefings take place. They speak in acronyms and code words that the public has never heard and, God (and the FBI) willing, never will hear."

Finding and touching key members of this Trumanite network will be difficult because the camouflage they wear is the best kind of camouflage. They are a subset of the most abundant part of government, and as such they are almost impossible to individually spot and verify simply because there are so many who basically appear like and work at similar locations as non-targets and neutrals. Here again we see how important the role of the non-combatant underground can be in helping the discovery and exposure of the individuals of the Trumanite network.

However, once discovered we must ask if it is worth the risk of targeting an individual? The true answer to that question is that it is rarely worth the investment and risk to target them. There are exceptions that should be targeted as soon as possible, but most are no more important to the State than the violent police mentioned earlier. Most will be replaced by another Trumanite before they can assume room temperature, and investing that much work and risk into a target that will be instantly replaced is not wise. We should always do a cost/benefit analysis when selecting targets, and again the non-combatant underground can play a critical role in that process. We'll need to have a good idea of what they do, who they work for and with, can they be easily replaced, and can we reach them with alternative methods better suited to our friend-saboteurs network. After all, a powerful murderous bureaucrat who is in the middle of a massive mental breakdown due to a carefully crafted gaslight operation is more valuable to us than a simple dead body.

Once again, when you look through that eyepiece and see a Trumanite they won't look like Adolf Hitler or Hannibal Lecter, but just keep in mind that their words and actions rain death upon the innocent, while the worst part of their day is sitting in traffic trying to escape the Beltway to get to their McMansion in the suburbs. Before you feel sorry for that State Department slug, do a StartPage image search of the children they murdered this week. Then realize that if no one steps up and stops them, they will kill by proxy again and again and again. However, always remember how these people reacted when Michael Hastings exposed one of them to the public while planning to expose more. Now imagine what their reaction would be if we targeted six Trumanites in one day. If you think the LAPD went nuts when Dorner killed a few coproaches, you won't believe how the dirt on the Hill in DC will react when Uruks start dropping in Mordor, and the same goes in every other capital city around the world.

(3-3) Non-Human Targets

Garnering less immediate reaction from governments, but possibly having a greater long term effect, will be the targeting of non-humans, including both the physical infrastructure and the corporate supports of the State. In these operations the individual warriors can work hand in hand with trusted non-combatant members of the underground. Ideally there should be friend-saboteurs working with hackers and other members of the underground to expose flaws in corporate security and weaknesses in key places like the communications infrastructure and the electrical grids.

(3-3.1) Targeting Infrastructure

The problem with targeting infrastructure is that it's a blade that cuts in all directions. In one sense, much of the faith the general public holds in the State rests upon its ability to provide roads, electricity, public water and sewer, and other such services. If they appear to slowly break down and the State is shown incapable or unwilling to keep them functional, then faith in the State is eroded. However if "terrorists" can be blamed for power outages and system failures the State can use the outages to increase tyranny and oppression. Knowing this, government agents have been documented over and over attacking their own citizenry and infrastructure for the express purpose of using these attacks as an excuse to gain more power over the people, thus we have the phrase "false flag event" to describe such actions. Yet again, that oppression gives rise to more resistance especially when the aboveground activists focus on the rise of oppression and show that the "terrorism" is just an excuse of the State to produce more tyranny. Ideally if the "terrorism" that actually causes the outages can be linked to government agents, it can be a propaganda victory for the forces of liberty, or it can just lead to more oppression. That means any strike against infrastructure is a delicate dance between success and failure, depending on so many variable that no one can calculate a guaranteed outcome. Of course, calculation problems never stop government actors from barging ahead.

Perhaps the perfect solution would be to stage a false flag event and frame government agents for the attack. Or even better, to bait a government agent to commit and bungle a false flag so that it could be exposed as such by the aboveground activists. That sounds almost impossible, but if it could be done it would truly be a grand accomplishment. FBI agents do the equivalent of this all the time in America, as they lure some mentally challenged desperate Muslim or militia member into a cockamamie plot that the FBI then uses as an excuse to arrest more Muslims or militia members.

The best practice, when it comes to a direct strike on infrastructure, may be to coordinate the timing with some other event. The main stream media is not good at following more than one major developing story, so an infrastructure failure could be used to distract coverage from some other event or the other way around.

(3-3.2) Targeting Crony Corporations

Many avid hunters dream of taking a safari, hunting the big game, taking down an African cape buffalo or an Alaskan grizzly bear. Likewise the fisherman may have dreams of bounding across Atlantic waves on a fishing boat with an 800 pound blue marlin on hook. It all sounds very romantic and brings to mind great manly men of the past like Ernest Hemingway or John Huston, sucking down Cohiba cigars while swirling cognac.

The reality of hunting and fishing is much different when you do it to stay alive. Survival and sustenance hunting and fishing typically don't depend on big game, and the further you are from drama and conflict the better chance you have of feeding the mouths that depend on your success. For this reason survival and sustenance hunting and fishing are more likely to focus on rabbits, squirrels, minnows, and catfish than any big game. This is hunting from necessity not entertainment.

The same is true when we think of fighting the State by taking on the corporate wing of the Dragon. We may all dream of sinking our lance deep in the heart of the military industrial complex or the banking cartels by striking some famous member of the Rothschild or Rockefeller families, or bagging a descendant of the House of Saxe-Coburg and Gotha, but we must live in the real world where even the mention of their wealth and power make people think you're crazy. They are the untouchables, and it's pure suicide to chase them.

No, we are fighting for survival and sustenance. Someday when the State is in its death throes, we will hunt the big game. But today, while the State is relatively healthy, we must hunt that which can be taken.

In 2014 a documentary by Tonje Hessen Schei was released titled Drone. That film contains an interview with a man named Andy Von Flotow, founder of the government surveillance drone supplier Insitu. Headquartered in Bingen, Washington USA, Insitu was a small company that was eventually absorbed by its long-time partner Boeing. In that brief interview Von Flotow makes several disturbing statements but toping it off he brags; "War is an opportunity to do business." This little slice of truth shows the nature of the people who facilitate the wholesale slaughter of humans for profit and power. Echoing what Major General Smedley Butler said in his 1935 book titled War Is a Racket, Von Flotow proudly admits his guilt in the crimes Butler described, and Smedley Butler was a man who knew about war. By the end of his career, Butler had received nineteen medals, five for heroism. He received the Medal of Honor twice, was one of only three Americans to be awarded both the Marine Corps Brevet Medal and the Medal of Honor, and was the only Marine ever to be awarded the Brevet Medal and two Medals of Honor, all for separate actions. Von Flotow has also made his contribution to war but has made a fortune in the process, so targeting him now would be like that old saying; Why close the barn door after the horse done run off. But a lesson can be learned from the man and the small company he founded. When Von Flotow founded Insitu, the focus of the company was in the development of unmanned weather reconnaissance vehicles, it wasn't until 2003 when Von Flotow and Insitu shifted to military applications. The time to slam the barn door on Von Flotow and Insitu would have been between that shift to militarism in 2003 and Insitu being swallowed by Boeing around 2008.

The idea of a corporation sharing the guilt of war with governments is hard for some people to accept until they make the whole connection between governments, the banking cartels, and the military industrial complex.

Some will say that what the corporations do in supplying governments through military contracts is no different than what the rum manufacture does in selling rum. It's not the rum makers fault when someone drinks rum, drives their car, and kills someone. But has Bacardi Limited ever sent company representatives into Alcoholics Anonymous meetings with rum samples? Do Bacardi sales representatives get a bonus in their wages based on increases in drunk driving death statistics? We know from a wide variety of inside sources including former US presidents, former high ranking military officers, and former leaders in the corporate world, that select corporations directly lobby for war in a wide range of ways.

Then there's the problem of choice and intent. As Kant teaches us, intent is the basis of judging an action. It's almost never the case that a man buys a bottle of rum with the full intent and purpose of getting drunk and killing someone. That's not to say the drunk should be excused for his actions and his poor choices, but he never intended to kill, and Bacardi didn't sell him the rum knowing ahead of time that he would kill. After all, the vast majority of rum drinkers never kill anyone. However the modern weapons of war are sold to governments exclusively, knowing full and well how they will be used. When Raytheon developed "millimeter wave source weapons" it wasn't so people could relax on a beach and enjoy a sunset, it was so government agents could use the equivalent of a cattle prod to move the human herds, and to single out individuals for direct punishment or death. Coupled with the fact that the decision makers in these corporations are the very same people who place the politicians in their offices, and as we have seen, the corporation decision-makers know that "War is an opportunity to do business." Therefore we can establish both choice and intent when we judge the corporate leaders that not only supply the means of war but encourage the decision to engage in those wars.

Now let's consider one more way Bacardi's rum sales to the public are different from Raytheon's relationship to governments. Setting aside whatever questionable business practices Bacardi Limited may or may not be guilty of, Bacardi's primary product is produced and consumed through voluntary market interactions with the general public. When Raytheon develops a product for warfare, even the original research funding is provided by governments and originally stolen from people through taxation.

So Bacardi primarily depends on voluntary market activity while Raytheon depends on taxation and influence buying. Without dedicating a whole paragraph to the international banking cartels, suffice to say, the military industrial complex and governments who engage in war never act without the involvement of the banking elite. So those corporate and banking executives who profit from war and death by guiding governments into war for the purpose of profits, are guilty of the murder that comes from their wars, yet the financial burden of those wars are involuntarily carried on the backs of taxpayers. Therefore we see that war is a racket and the racketeers are the corporate and banking executives, the politicians, and the Trumanites that profit from wars, whereas the victims of war are the dead on all sides, and the taxpayers who are forced to pay for it all. Bacardi Limited, as we have shown, carries no such burden of guilt.

Just like Bacardi Limited is used only as an example here, so is Raytheon just one example of the military industrial complex. And it's worth noting in the metaphor of the hunter, Raytheon is not an easy catch like a rabbit, a squirrel or a catfish, but they are not a bull elephant either. Raytheon is simply one scale on that dragon we call the State.

4. COMMITTEES OF VIGILANCE

(4-1) Vigilante Justice

Few things have been systematically and intentionally demonized more than "vigilante justice" and leading that witch hunt for the last century has been the Hollywood entertainment industry. At the height of Hollywood cowboy movies during the mid-twentieth century, the American entertainment industry was almost incapable of producing anything referencing the "Old West" that didn't feature either a demonization of stateless wild Indians on a murderous rampage with the helpless settlers saved by the military, or a lynch mob attempting to hang some innocent man, with a brave sheriff saving the day. This "Wild West" narrative permeated not only motion pictures and television, but almost every work of fiction about the West written during the twentieth century.

This simple fact should cause any free thinking person to ask why there would be such uniform condemnation of anything. Any person who owns their own mind should immediately suspect any narrative that is so one-sided, so dramatically portrayed, and pushed so heavily by the same people who support the State at every turn including justifying and glorifying the horrors of war. Consider the twentieth century Hollywood version of any portrayal of any historical event, and consider their amazing propensity to get almost every detail wrong, and you begin to see that something is rotten in Hollywood's universal condemnation of vigilantism.

When a free thinking person realizes propaganda on such a grand scale, that person should immediately ask why so much effort has been expended on that one topic. But of course, we know the reason. Vigilante justice is the single most dangerous thing the State faces. To start with, the State claims a monopoly on justice, but vigilante justice is the only way to achieve true justice. The alternative to vigilante justice is the perverted version of justice that the State supplies, and we know what that kind of distorted justice is, and what kind of a sick and twisted society it produces. This is the reason that every time the State has expanded and engulfed stateless societies such as; pre-Cromwell Celtic-Christian Ireland, pre-English-invasion Scotland, pre-English Australia, native North America excluding the Mesoamerican empires, pre-1800 Scot-Irish Appalachia, the American West prior to the post-Civil War expansion of the State, and the Zomia of upland southeast Asia, the very first thing the State does is to outlaw vigilante justice and inflict its monopoly of State justice.

This is the situation in which we find ourselves today. The State has systematically denied justice while demonizing aspects of true justice. It has, through its puppets in the media, the schools, and the clergy, taught that revenge is uncivilized and barbaric or even sinful. Justice is redefined as whatever the current government decides in each individual case. Recompense is paid to the government and almost never to the victim. The government, not the victim, dictates the punishment and then the government imprisons and punishes the accused perpetrator behind closed doors and out of public sight. The government, through immoral taxation, forces victims and innocent bystanders to pay for the incarceration process, all the time making false assurances of safety and security. Then it arbitrarily releases criminals back into society that are often more violent and dangerous than when they were first incarcerated.

And finally in desperation, as its failures become more and more obvious, governments begins redefining crime so that almost any normal peaceful activity can be criminalized and punished. And yet people fear vigilante justice. It would be comical if it weren't so tragic.

If we understand that everything we've been taught about vigilante justice is false, and we know the State is incapable of producing justice while it attempts to enforce its monopoly control to prevent vigilante justice, logically we should know that we need to revisit what we believe about justice.

True justice has a number of components. Among these are:

- Assurance – Knowing that this perpetrator will never do this crime to this victim again.

- Recompense – A return of, or a monetary compensation for what was stolen or damaged.

- Revenge – Personally inflicting or witnessing the infliction of suffering upon the perpetrator, above and beyond the original damages, for the purpose of easing the trauma of the victim and to show the perpetrator and the community that this behavior is unacceptable.

Scholars who study this topic have endlessly discussed how these systems have functioned for extended periods without government interference. They've also shown that stateless societies very quickly develop systems to ensure true justice, but until now one thing has been missing from the conversation. That is the failure of non-state justice systems to defend people from the crime gangs that operate governments. When stateless people are invaded by a government those people respond in several ways, but the one thing we don't see is vigilante groups treating government employees and State actors as the crime gangs that they are. This is something we can address. We simply begin forming committees of vigilance and, one at a time on local levels, we begin prosecuting those who act on behalf of the international crime gang known as the State. We start with the ones we can reach. We touch those who can be touched. We get better each time we act, and we weaken the State with every small strike. Eventually we can touch those who were out of reach before and at some point we reach the untouchables.

(4-2) Forming Committees of Vigilance

A committee of vigilance should be a secret unit, formed of like-minded friends, made up of whatever combination of dedicated underground activists you have available. The committee should concern itself with one thing; justice. What sports teams are doing or how the weather has been can be discussed anywhere with anyone, but when a committee of vigilance meets they should do so with one purpose and one purpose only; to seek and deliver justice. When individual members of a vigilance committee are found to constantly bring up outside issues or distractions, that member should be excluded from the meetings. Natural leaders will likely develop but anyone who begins to shift the focus of the committee to self-glorification should be excluded from the meetings. If possible, the committee should be made up of individual warriors and trusted non-combatant members of the underground, with the individual warriors acting as the enforcement wing. A committee doesn't have to include an enforcement wing, but without one it becomes an exercise in academics. That's not necessarily a bad thing, if the committee can eventually develop an enforcement wing. In that way, a committee can be a kind of teaching opportunity for activists who feel the need to move into the individual warrior classification. Once the local committee connects with a network of vigilance committees, members of the enforcement wing or wings can be shared, as their specialties may be unique.

A committee of vigilance shouldn't include every underground activist in an area, unless you have a serious shortage of activists. The committee should be very selective of who is allowed in, and who they communicate with on committee business outside of the committee. Whenever possible a committee should seek to interact with other committees, forming a distributed network, ideally spreading globally. It shouldn't be a hard rule to exclude aboveground activists, however everyone involved in a committee of vigilance should clearly understand the risks involved. Authoritarians on every level of the State will, as soon as they are aware of us, begin referring to us as terrorists. This is the reason such an emphasis on secrecy should be employed.

The primary purpose of a committee of vigilance should be to develop target lists, hold target review hearings, do target risk/benefit analysis, and make final decisions on the fate of the target, then communicate that decision to the enforcement wing. The secondary purpose of a committee of vigilance should be to discuss potential new members of the underground, develop trust lists and contact lists (both to be kept encrypted and secured) and expand network connections. Additionally every member of a committee of vigilance should have a clear understanding of the concept of mission creep and the committee should be constantly self-examining to assure that mission creep doesn't slip into your activities.

5. FUNDING

Compared to funding a State based justice system, vigilante justice is practically free and usually funds itself. Again, stateless societies tend to solve problems like funding on their own very quickly. However getting a committee of vigilance started and functional under the current circumstance will cost a small amount of money. That fact should not prevent us from moving ahead in the process. Local groups can move as slow as they need to, so long as they are moving in the right direction. Always remember, we must keep our goal as winning the long fight, not solving an immediate issue. Moving slowly but directly towards a goal is better than moving rapidly in the wrong direction. So a lack of funding should never be an excuse to sit idly by doing nothing. Be creative and do what you can do with the resources you have.

That said, since we know that war is paid for through the stolen money that governments extract from the working masses, we then know that the profits of war are filthy lucre and are not the rightful property of those corporations, bankers, executives, politicians, and Trumanites who possess them. So let's face the facts, the filthy lucre of the State lies in abundance for those brave enough to walk into the Dragon's lair and take it, but walking out of that lair with the gold requires more than bravery.

(5.1) Filthy Lucre

Filthy Lucre: money gained in a dishonest or dishonorable way.

That's the simple yet accurate definition of filthy lucre. The money itself takes on no magical residue of its ill-gotten past. Money is inanimate and is not to blame for human actions; therefore it can carry with it no guilt of past deeds. Stolen money in the possession of thieves, robbers, crony corporations, crony executives, crony bankers, politicians, and other such scum is unowned property and available for rightful homesteading. Additionally, since these crime gang members are routinely guilty of either direct aggression on the innocent, or are guilty of aggression through proxy, none of the property they have come to possess under any circumstances is protected by natural rights theory and is therefore rightfully unowned. It's part of the duty of a properly functioning justice system to acquire such funds and utilize those funds to accomplish the three aspects of justice listed above, namely; assurance, recompense, and revenge. Starting with assurance, we cannot assure victims that the robbery won't continue so long as the crime gang known as the State continues to function. So one of our priorities in dealing with filthy lucre should be to safely extract as much as possible from the criminals and repurpose it for our cause of ending the State.

Methods of liberating the filthy lucre of the State will vary widely, according to the skill levels of activists and the opportunities presented in our interaction with State actors. However it is imperative that we maintain our principles. We cannot terrorize the innocent, and the families of State actors are not guilty by default. We must be surgical and precise in our handling of State actors, and whenever possible we should stay anonymous and keep the purpose of our cause hidden for as long as possible.

6. WINNING: THE LESSON OF ALGERIA

Algeria was invaded then violently and mercilessly conquered by France in the 1830s. For over one hundred years Algeria was a military colony where land was stolen from its traditional owners and handed out to waves of European immigrants, who were then favored by the French legal system over the indigenous Muslim and Jewish Algerians. All that changed on November 1, 1954, when guerrilla fighters began a war that lasted until France was humiliated and forced to resign in 1962. During that brief war from 1954 until 1962, France was so devastated that France itself almost erupted in a civil war. And all of this was made possible by a small group of irregular warriors called the National Liberation Front.

By 1960 the French force in Algeria was in excess of 300,000 highly trained combat troops supplied with the most modern equipment. At its peak of power during the war, the National Liberation Front numbered something less than 30,000 fighters, poorly equipped with only light weapons when they had weapons at all. At one point in the city of Algiers, the clandestine warfare organization was comprised of approximately 1,200 armed men, and 4,500 persons unarmed. Yet the Algerians soundly defeated the French. They did so by using strike-and-run tactics, by avoiding open conflict, and by hiding in plain sight. At one point a major leader of the NLF had his operation headquarters only a few hundred meters from a French stronghold in Algiers. The French could neither see nor understand their enemy, so the French never had a chance.

As the respected French authority on the Algerian war and on irregular warfare, Roger Trinquier stated; "We know that the sine qua non of victory in modern warfare is the unconditional support of a population. According to Mao Tse-tung, it is as essential to the combatant as water to the fish. Such support may be spontaneous, although that is quite rare and probably a temporary condition. If it doesn't exist, it must be secured by every possible means, the most effective of which is terrorism." When Trinquier speaks of terrorism, he is speaking of a situation where local fighters harass both authority and the civilian population, and at the same time the authority is unable to maintain security for the local population. So the population both fears the terrorism and hate the authority for failing to provide security.

In our version of ethics based irregular warfare, the attacks would be on authoritarian individuals and on infrastructure, but never directly on the civilian population. As attacks increase in number and effectiveness, the population more and more will blame authorities while authorities have no one to "crack down" on except the innocent civilian population. Reading Roger Trinquier's analysis of the Algerian war and his assessments of the French Indochina war are fascinating and informative, but not completely applicable to our purposes. The two assumptions of authoritarians, in regards to warfare, is that either geography must be controlled or populations must be controlled, with the goal to control both.

We must reject this. We can never attempt to control either. Our path to victory and the death of the State will rely upon our practice of never directly engaging the might of the State while always respecting the lives and property of the civilian population. Whenever possible, we should avoid terrorizing the public or inciting panic in any way. Whenever our target must be a public one, that target should be hated, otherwise don't let it look like a hit. We must never incite sympathy for the devil.

The final lesson of Algeria is the lesson of every revolution throughout history. When the French abandoned Algeria, the old far away tyrant was replaced by a new local tyrant, and the cycle of the State continued. This is what revolutions always produce. Therefore we must not engage in revolution. We must strike, we must agitate, we must provoke, but mostly we must provide the framework for the aboveground network to teach and advertise a better option than the slavery of the State until the day that the market demand shifts and people stop wanting the State.

9. MEET TOM SMITH

Tom works at the Pentagon, and Tom loves his job. Last month he moved to a window office that looks out toward the lagoon, so he can watch the boats coming in and out of the marina. It took Tom 18 years to get where he is, and he knows he deserves this job. Tom has a nice place out in Warrenton. It's a hard hour drive each way without traffic, and there's always traffic, but it's worth it to get his family out of the Beltway and into a nice area out in the country. Tom makes the sacrifice for his kids, and he feels good about that. Tom's wife, Betty volunteers at the kid's school, so most mornings Tom and Betty load the kids in the car and they all ride together. It's just down the street on the way to Lee Highway. Betty's mother comes by the school in the afternoon and gives them a ride home. It's nice to have family nearby.

Most mornings Tom goes down Faiquier Road, drops the wife and kids at the LDS church school, and then stops down the street at the Exxon to fill up before hitting the Lee Highway and heading into the grind. Sometimes Tom cheats, but don't tell Betty. There's a donut place just around the corner and sometimes Tom slips over and grabs a coffee and an apple fritter.

The truth is, Tom doesn't cheat "sometimes". Tom cheats and gets a coffee and a fritter every Friday, but Tom feels like he has earned it. Tom has worked hard and made sacrifices to get where he is and to achieve this life he's made for himself.

One Friday morning, as Tom pulled into the donut place, he saw the drive-through was backed up with some kind of utility truck that clearly shouldn't have tried to go through the drive-through. No problem, Tom just nosed into one of the open parking spaces and hopped out of his car. Then everything in Tom's world changed.

He hadn't seen it before but a white utility van was right at his rear bumper and the slide door was opening. Tom felt a heavy hand on his left shoulder and another strong hand grabbed his right arm.

"Come with me Mr. Smith, we have some questions. This won't take but a moment and you'll be free to go on your way."

The van door finished opening and a man stepped out, "No problems now Mr. Smith, this can be quick and easy and you can go on to work."

In a flash they were all in the van and the door was closed. There were more men inside.

"I apologize sir, but this is absolutely necessary, I can assure you." said one of the men as he began frisking and searching Tom. No doubt about it Tom was scared, but somewhere in Tom's mind he was justifying what was happening. These men seemed like agency men. They seemed very professional. Tom asked a few questions trying to determine who they worked for and what their purpose was, but there were no direct answers.

"Don't worry sir; we have no intention of harming you. We only have some questions and some things to show you and you can go on to work." The contents of Tom's pockets and his phone were put in a small tray. One of the men took Toms key fob and Tom's phone and handed it out the window to someone Tom couldn't see. Then the van started moving.

Over the next twenty minutes or so, the van was on some highway while the men stripped Tom to his underwear and socks. Then he was placed on a small metal seat that jutted from the van wall. When the van stopped a man in the back of the van that had been doing something on a laptop spoke up; "We're in." He barked. The laptop was spun around. There was an image of a small child's body, cut in half and partly burned. "There are some things you need to look at and then we'll have some questions for you, Mr. Smith."

For the next few minutes a little slide show was displayed for Tom. Pictures of dead children, an old woman torn apart but still struggling to live, a wedding party blown to bits by a Hellfire strike, before and after pictures of an upscale home in Syria, now nothing but rubble, and finally a close up picture of a small boy that had been tortured with wire pliers. Then the pictures changed. Here was Tom standing at his mailbox. Here was Tom walking out of the church building. Now a picture of Tom sitting in traffic. Finally a close up picture of Tom standing on his back porch, sipping orange juice from a glass, except there was a bright red dot on his chest.

"Mr. Smith, it's important for you to face what you really do for a living." stated one of the men. One of the other's drew very close to Tom's face and said quietly, "Wouldn't it be sad if something like this happened in Warrenton? That little boy is about the same age as your son."

The first man pulled the other man back and said, "Now there's no need to worry about something like that, Mr. Smith. We would never let that happen." The laptop image changed and Tom realized he was looking at his bank's homepage. Over the next few minutes Tom, with the help of his captors, moved money out of Tom's accounts into a Bitcoin account. Then the van began moving again. Tom was allowed to get dressed as the van moved down the highway. No one spoke.

When the van stopped again, Tom was fully dressed. The first man that had grabbed Tom's arm in the beginning spoke clear and slow, "Now here's what happens next. Your car is here waiting for you. You will be free to go. You will not speak about this to anyone. We want that to be vividly clear. You don't want us to come back to visit you again because we won't be nice the next time. When you step out of this van a kind of timer will start. That timer will tick for exactly six months from today. Then that timer will pop your name up on someone's schedule. You need to have quit your job by that day. Otherwise a process will start that can't be reversed. You have six months to get out of your government job and you must never work for the government or any government contractor again, otherwise very bad things will happen. And again, you need to stay quiet about what happened today, otherwise what will happen Mr. Smith?"

There was a pause. "Mr. Smith, I need for you to say it. What will happen if you talk about this?"

Tom slowly spoke, "Bad ..."

"Bad things, Mr. Smith. Very bad things."

The van door opened and the man handed Tom the items from the tray. Tom stepped out into the light, while the van door slammed and the van drove away. Tom looked around. It took a second, but Tom knew where he was. Tom was standing in front of his car in the Dick's Sporting Goods parking lot just down Columbia Pike from the Pentagon. His key fob and phone were on the hood of his car.

END: Part 3 ETHICS BASED SELECTIVE IRREGULAR WARFARE

YOU MIGHT ALSO BE INTERESTED IN:

A VONU GUIDE TO FIREARMS
by josiah warren

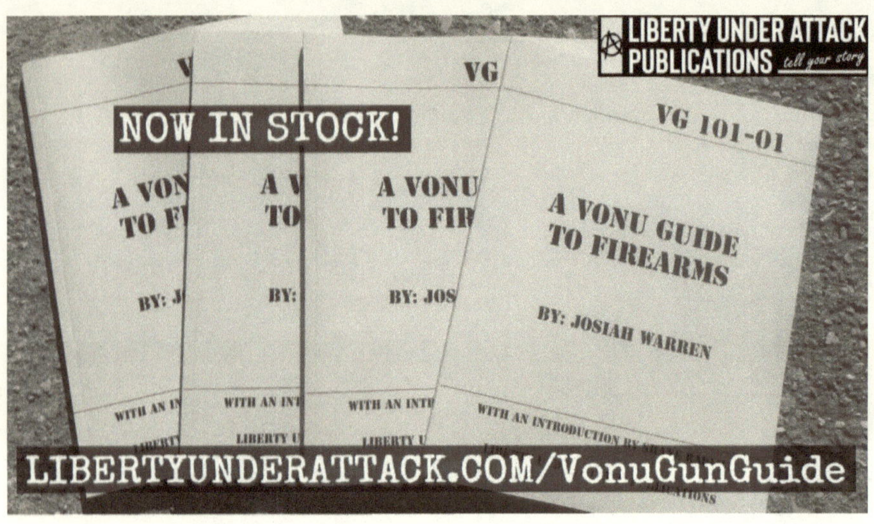

- FULL COLOR, special magazine-style book
- FEATURES An Introduction to Vonu by Shane Radliff
- TRANSCRIPT for Gun Printing 101 "course" with IvanTheTroll (originally a Vonu Podcast episode)
- LEARN how to select a firearm, to build or to buy, safety, firing, & maintenannce, purchasing gun parts with bitcoin, & more!

LIBERTY UNDER ATTACK PUBLICATIONS *tell your story*

24. **An Illusive Phantom of Hope: A Critique of Reformism** by Kyle Rearden (Audiobook/Anthology)
25. **The Production of Security** by Gustave de Molinari (Audiobook)
26. **Are Cops Constitutional?** by Roger Roots (Audiobook)
27. **Argumentation Ethics: An Anthology** by Hans-Herman Hoppe et al (Anthology)
28. **Just Below The Surface: A Guide to Security Culture** by Kyle Rearden (Audiobook/Paperback)
29. **Sedition, Subversion, and Sabotage, Field Manual No. 1: A Three Part Solution to the State** by Ben Stone (Paperback/Audiobook)
30. **#agora** by anonymous (Paperback/Audiobook)
31. **Vonu: A Strategy for Self-Liberation** by Shane Radliff (Paperback)
32. **Second Realm: Book on Strategy** by Smuggler and XYZ (Paperback/Audiobook)
33. **Vonu: The Search for Personal Freedom** by Rayo (Special Paperback Reprint/Audiobook)
34. **Vonu: The Search for Personal Freedom, Part 2 [Letters From Rayo]** (Paperback)
35. **Going Mobile** by Tom Marshall (Paperback/Audiobook)
36. **Anarchist to Abolitionist: A Bad Quaker's Journey** by Ben Stone
37. **Brushfire, A Thriller** by Matthew Wojtecki (Paperback/Audiobook)
38. **2048 (A BRUSHFIRE THRILLER)** by Matthew Wojtecki
39. **VonuLife, March 1973** by Rayo et al (Paperback)
40. **Ocean Freedom Notes** by Jim Stumm, Rayo, et al (Paperback)
41. **The Big Book of Secret Hiding Places** by Jack Luger (Paperback)
42. **The Invention of Evil** by Henry Jones (Paperback/Kindle)
43. **Low Cost Living Notes** by Jim Stumm et al (Paperback/Kindle)
44. **Survival Gardening Notes** by Jim Stumm et al (Paperback/Kindle)
45. **The Permanent Floating Voluntary Society** by Kerry Thornley (Paperback/Kindle)
46. **A Vonu Guide to Firearms** by Josiah Warren & Shane Radliff (Paperback)

Visit <u>LibertyUnderAttack.com</u> for discounted bundles, privacy tools, **and more!**